SOCIAL JUSTICE

BOWLING GREEN STUDIES
IN APPLIED PHILOSOPHY

Volume IV - 1982

SOCIAL JUSTICE

BOWLING GREEN STUDIES IN APPLIED PHILOSOPHY
Volume IV - 1982

Edited by the Faculty of the Department of Philosophy
Bowling Green State University

Michael Allen
Thomas W. Attig
Michael Bradie
Ramona T. Cormier
Robert P. Goodwin
Louis I. Katzner
Richard H. Lineback
Loy Littlefield
Fred D. Miller, Jr.
Jeffrey Paul
Michael H. Robins
Donald Rothberg
Donald W. Scherer
Robert Strikwerda
James D. Stuart
Fredric C. Young

PRINCIPAL EDITORS

Michael Bradie and David Braybrooke

The Applied Philosophy Program
Bowling Green State University
Bowling Green, Ohio

170
5678

Published by   The Applied Philosophy Program
               Bowling Green State University
               Bowling Green, Ohio 43403

ISBN 0-935756-05-1 hardback

86-9691

Typesetting by   The Philosophy Documentation Center
                 Bowling Green State University

CONTENTS

PREFACE

This is the fourth volume of the Bowling Green Studies in Applied Philosophy. These studies are devoted to the investigation of the implications of theories of metaphysics, epistemology, and ethics, as well as the human sciences for social problems which require rational planning and decision making.

Applied philosophy is not a recent innovation. Its practical objective is set forth in a passage by Aristotle in the *Nicomachean Ethics*: "We are inquiring not in order to know what virtue is, but to become good." Theoretical inquiry has an essential place in the total enterprise, but the ultimate concern is with the implications of theory for human action.

The papers in this volume were originally presented at a conference on Social Justice, held at Bowling Green State University on May 7-8, 1982. The conference, the fourth in an annual series, was held under the auspices of the Applied Philosophy Program at Bowling Green State University, and supported in part by a grant from the National Endowment for the Humanities.

The keynote paper, by David Braybrooke, argues for the need to develop a consensus about social justice which will make the concept of social justice fully practical. This is to be achieved by demanding what Braybrooke calls "full currency," namely, an account of justice which can be understood by ordinary people, and which yields determinate results on real world issues, results that, in turn, accord with what ordinary people think about social justice. A fully current account should also attract steady support from ordinary people, whatever their present privileges. Most accounts of justice fail to satisfy these conditions. The strategy of Braybrooke's approach is first to get people to agree on what are departures from justice and then to get them to agree on a concept of social justice which seeks to keep such departures in check. Braybrooke suggests that human needs play an important role in such a concept of justice because people are especially vulnerable to abuses of power when these needs are not met. James Sterba, commenting on Braybrooke's paper, argues that Braybrooke's own view does not satisfy his conditions of full currency. He suggests trying to form popular versions of the views Braybrooke rejects; and argues that once this is done, a general consensus on practical action will emerge regardless of the particular account of social justice from which one starts.

The rest of the papers fall into four categories: justice and equality, distributive justice, foundations of justice, and problems in applied justice.

In the section on justice and equality, James Fishkin outlines a dilemma that faces theories of justice which try to take into account the interests of future generations, and he proposes a principle which makes use of both identity specific and identity independent considerations in order to avoid it. Michael McDonald argues that both contemporary liberal and conservative concepts of justice are morally inadequate. McDonald suggests that, by deemphasizing, in favor of communitarian considerations, the role of the interests of rationally self-sufficient agents, a more acceptable concept of justice may be formulated. Sidney Axinn argues that the equal protection clause of the 14th Amendment should be applied to the collective effect of a group of laws rather than to the effect of a particular law.

In the section on distributive justice, Jennifer Hochschild examines the perceptions of poor people about justice. She concludes that the poor are egalitarians with respect to personal and political justice, but are non-egalitarians with respect to economic justice. Christopher Morris argues that a non-egalitarian, liberal, individualist case can be made for a coercive redistribution of goods from haves to havenots. Hugo Bedau points out that classical theories of justice and some recent libertarian theories fail to provide a role for the satisfaction of human needs. But, he argues, any adequate theory of social justice must be designed to identify and explain how and why human needs should be satisfied.

In the section on foundations of justice, Andrew Altman argues that no theory of justice derivable from non-controversial first premises is forthcoming. Social philosophers should thus focus on bringing about practical compromises to ethical disagreements rather than the pursuit of theoretical will-o-the-wisps. Larry Thomas argues for social libertarianism on the grounds that societies which promote pluralism and individualism are more in tune with a basic psychological need for self-respect. Ferdinand Schoeman argues for a conception of rights that is social rather than individualistic.

In the section on problems in applied justice, David Hoekema argues that the present tax system in the United States which assumes that fair taxation involves (1) the equitable distribution of the costs of government, and (2) a progressive income tax, is, in fact, unjust. In its stead he proposes a tax on wealth and consumption rather than income. Brian Schrag addresses the problem of distribution of primary care physicians in the United States. He argues that such distribution should be based on need; the distribution turns out, in a sense, to be egalitarian. Hardy Jones raises a number of disturbing issues about the relationship between a potential donor and his bodily organs. In particular, he argues that, in many cases, consent of the donor is not a necessary condition for the moral permissibility of organ donation.

We wish again to thank Patricia Bressler for her efforts in making the conference a success and for her contributions to the preparation of this manuscript.

MAKING JUSTICE PRACTICAL

David Braybrooke

No doubt present social discontents do not arise solely because of the absence of a consensus upon social justice; nor would arriving at such a consensus cure all the discontents. Whatever we do about justice, it is going to be uncomfortable to adjust to shortages of energy. There is, however, a sort of unrest that is continually manifested in union demands for higher wages, continually rising, without limit in principle; and that blocks any serious attempt to control inflation by the sort of policy recommended by economists who recognize the political aspects of inflation, namely, an incomes policy. This sort of unrest, I think, could be reduced, even in the end eliminated, if we managed to achieve, Canada for its part and the United States for its, a consensus upon social justice. To do so, however, we shall have to bring the concept of justice down from the level of idealized philosophical discussion; we shall have to make the concept fully practical, and to do so, we shall have to make it fully current.

By full currency, I mean giving an account of justice that meets three tests:

First, the test of being readily understood by ordinary people, let us say, at least by people capable of reading comprehendingly most of the contents of a good newspaper;

Second, the test of giving determinate results, rejecting some policies and favoring others, on the issues actually encountered in the real world, and, moreover, of giving results that make sense of the ideas that ordinary people already have about justice;

Third, the test of attracting steady support from ordinary people, taking them as they are, in positions more or less privileged, and thus with different interests at stake in the *status quo*.

The third test we may expect to be the hardest to meet, even if we qualify it (as I shall) to apply only to people who are ready to justify their agreement or disagreement by appeal to relevant reasons. Most of the accounts of justice now in circulation manage as well, however, to fail one or the other of the first two tests, more or less badly.

All accounts of justice that make use of the notion of utility fail the first and second tests. This is so not just because utility, even before its refinement by economists and decision-theorists, was, and was from the time that the felicific calculus was first proposed, a technical concept that has no use in ordinary life. It is so because the concept has no application in practice to the choice of social policies and never will, apart from serving as a convenient device for making certain points that can be made better with more familiar concepts, or apart from serving as a sort of variable that in practice is replaced by those familiar concepts. In truth, the notion must be conceded to have played an effective historical role in resolving the paradox of value (how can water cost so little and diamonds so much, when the first is so much more useful than the second?); in preventing people from making mistakes like Hobbes's in arguing from a partial coincidence of a monarch's interests with his subjects' to an identity of interests; in justifying progressive income taxation by explaining why taking $100,000 from someone with $200,000 in income is not equivalent to taking $1,000 from each of 100 people each with $2,000 in income. All these points are better made, however, at least once they are discovered, without resort to the notion of utility, and by talking instead about (for example) people's capacity to meet their needs or to advance their interests, beyond meeting their needs, in getting more income.

It is an illusion to suppose that we can draw up utility functions for the people affected by social policies. Even if we had a fully satisfactory procedure for drawing up utility functions for single persons, taking them one at a time, which we don't, we are not actually going to do it in even a single case; it never has been done and it never will be. Moreover, were it done, we would, in the most promising case (following von Neumann's and Morgenstern's procedure) face intractable problems of interpersonal comparisons. We can, of course, make interpersonal comparisons relevant to questions of justice, but they are not precise comparisons, and they are not comparisons of utility. Theorists—economists or philosophers—who use the notion of utility continually forget these things, and continually overlook the fact that should anyone attempt to apply their theories, the information about utility is gong to be absent. People will resort instead to information about needs and provisions for needs, or about money incomes, or about marketbasket indices of real income. Information organized by such familiar concepts was the information used to apply utilitarianism to sanitary reform in London; it is the information that is used in lieu of utility whenever utility is brought forward for practical application. It would be better to bring forward the familiar concepts in the first place.

The leading contemporary accounts of justice also fail the first and second tests by making use of an idealized model in which some sort of idealized original position figures. I am using the term "original position" in a generalized way, to cover any status quo, hypothetical or historical (or both together), supposed itself to be free of injustice, and supposed therefore to offer suitable circumstances for initiating processes that will conform to justice if certain conditions, specified in the model, are adhered to. The position may be one in which, as with Rawls, agents choose the principles of justice behind a veil of ignorance; or one, as with Nozick, in which people confront the riches of nature without yet having appropriated or misappropriated anything; or one, as with Gauthier, in which fully-informed agents, identifiable with members of present-day society, proceed under conditions closer to Nozick's original position than to Rawls's to bargain about features of the social contract.[1] Philosophers themselves have some difficulty in understanding just how these models make the results arrived at in them compelling either in theory or in application. And how can they be applied if, as in Nozick's case, they require us to retrace the history of mankind in impossible detail to a position that cannot be uniquely identified anyway?[2] The hypothetical reasoning involved in the models is not just a complication that ordinary people find difficult to follow, though it is that; it inevitably opens up a gap between the account of justice and present-day facts. Ordinary people can appreciate that there is a gap without being able to tell just why it exists; so they, in the end rightly, must suspect the accounts of being to some degree irrelevant to present issues.

Finally, for present purposes, I note that all accounts of justice that rely upon pure procedural criteria alone for determining the distribution of income and wealth — of advantages in general — fail the second test. For procedures alone, certainly the procedures of competitive markets, do not forestall the development of end-results that conflict in themselves with ordinary intuitions about justice and that jeopardize keeping up the very procedures relied upon. Neither Nozick nor Gauthier, for example, provides against the possibility that one person, with a monopoly, let us say, in a very popular and easily marketable talent, could come by the aggregation of transactions individually legitimate to be entitled to 99 percent of the Gross or Net World Product. But end-results far short of that fantasy will raise disturbing questions about the provision for some people's needs and the jeopardy in which they and the procedures have been placed by the aggrandizements obtained by the people most successful under the procedures. It is no answer to this point to imply that everyone should be on his toes, fully engaged in the market everyday. If everyone were so, the procedures might turn out to be self-defeating notwithstanding; and on what grounds are even those with limited zeal for trading to be forced to be traders to protect themselves?

Most contemporary accounts, besides failing the first and second tests, fail the third one, too. Many readers have thought that Rawls's account, by leaving a gap between the agents in the original position, who do not know what privileges they may have in present-day society, and agents who are conscious of their privileges, fails to motivate people in the real world who would lose substantially by carrying out his principles. A much worse difficulty, in my view, is the fact that in the absence of a good empirical theory of incentives, people with present privileges can argue that the Difference Principle is already satisfied, since (so they say) the privileges are necessary to them as incentives for their (supposed) social contributions. Almost as bad is the difficulty that the application of Rawls's principles might require as much sacrifice of people's present positions, acquired under expectations of legitimate continuance, as the principle of utility ever would. However, Rawls's account is, in respect to the third test, much closer to being fully current, in spite of these difficulties, than Nozick's is. Appearances to the contrary notwithstanding, Nozick's account, if it were followed in practice, would require the most radical unsettling of the present distribution of wealth that anyone this side of Marxism has ever contemplated. All present holdings, we must hypothesize, are tainted to some degree by misappropriations in the past; all those misappropriations must be traced and their results undone. People will find it difficult to agree to doing this, not being able to foresee in most cases what they will lose or gain in the end, and not being convinced that justice requires going back to Attila the Hun and beyond to resuscitate long-superseded grievances. The amount of time and distraction that the research would demand is by itself a decisive objection, though subtler ones can be found. Gregory Kavka, examining closely[3] Nozick's Rectification Principle in a perspective much like James Fishkin's in the paper below, has shown in effect that Nozick faces a dilemma: Either he has to ascribe some value to people's simply existing and accept it that for them when their existence depends on past actions, however unjust, the Rectification Principle is vacuously satisfied; or he has to work out some procedure for hypothetical comparisons of people's condition with and without the effects of any questioned actions, in which case he loses any advantage that he purports to have over Rawls's and others' hypothetical constructions. Above, of course, I treated Nozick as in effect having no such advantage anyway, since his argument postulates an idealized original position in a hypothetical model, though a different position and a different model from Rawls's.

I am not saying that the accounts of justice rejected by my three tests are all of them rejected as beyond repair. Some of them are much closer, at least in certain features, to being fully current than others; and I shall in fact make use of something like Rawls's Difference Principle in my own attempt at full currency. Nor am I saying that being fully current is the only thing to be valued in an account of justice. On the contrary: a theory of justice can be very illuminating philosophically even if it flagrantly fails all three tests. Such is the case, for example, with Gauthier's account. It may not be fully current. It nevertheless shows us more — more than any other account so far of the relation between self-interest and morals — about the limits to which non-tuistic rational choice can be pushed in an effort to capture the chief points of morals for a theory of mutual advantage that itself begs no moral questions. This, and other achievements of these accounts, are not at issue in charging them with failing to be fully current.

Let me now set forth the main features of an account of justice that I claim does have full currency — or at least will, once it has been perfected. It is an account that (unlike many others) treats distributive justice in a unified perspective where other aspects of justice equally figure. It is an account that dispenses with the notion of utility in favor of the concept of needs and some related concepts. It is an account that keeps the actual status quo in the real world in view at all times, with impending transformations of it, rather than relying on hypothetical reasoning, an idealized model, and an original position very different from the status quo. It is an account that does not rely, anywhere, on pure procedural criteria alone; everywhere in it, procedures are subject to check, offset, and supersession by non-procedural criteria. Thus the account has some promise, by avoiding the objections that I have raised to other accounts of meeting the three tests; and I think that the extent to which it does meet them will emerge quite naturally and incidentally in the course of my exposition.

We begin with the actual status quo, the distribution of wealth, positions, and entitlements in (say) Canada or the United States today. For short, I shall often speak of the distribution of "advantages." Then we consider possible departures from this status quo — examples of departures that are already happening. To simplify exposition, I shall concentrate upon transactions, leaving aside many other sorts of departures, all of which raise questions about justice (which, fortunately, can be given parallel treatment): gifts; productive contributions; savings and dissavings; extortion; natural disasters; taxes; subsidies.

For the moment, I raise no questions about the status quo itself. I ask, what is just or unjust about transactions departing from it? There is, I think, remarkably firm and widespread agreement about the clear cases of injustice in transactions. A transaction is unjust when one party misrepresents the goods that he offers so that after the transaction the one who misrepresented gains, and the other party loses, relatively to the positions that the parties held in the status quo. Or a transaction is unjust when one party hands over the goods or performs the services agreed upon and the other hands over less or does less than agreed upon, perhaps nothing at all, so again the status quo has been changed to the advantage of one party and to the disadvantage of the other.

On the other hand, predictably enough, we regard a transaction as just if the two parties end up equally well off in comparison with their points of departure in the status quo. "Equally well off" is something judged to be such with a good deal of elasticity. We generally defer to the parties themselves: If they both consider that they have done equally well, we count them as doing so, though we find it hard to conceive (for example) how anyone could rationally pay so much money for a dusty stuffed owl. If one or the other party is dissatisfied after the event, we have, of course, to look around for other standards. We ask whether they have either of them changed their minds, which would explain the dissatisfaction consistently with holding the transaction to have been just; or whether either was misinformed, with the other taking advantage of the misinformation, which would make the transaction unjust, among other things by the failure of the equal results criterion; or whether the discrepancy in the value of the goods or services exchanged was so great, by ordinary standards, as to raise questions about the competence of either party to arrive at equal results. I do not underestimate the complications of individual cases, or the frequency with which people will disagree about them. Nevertheless, clear cases of transactions both just and unjust can be found; and there is general agreement not only about the judgments that they invite, but also about the considerations on which they rest, which are the same considerations to be brought up in discussions of the less certain cases.

Next, I point out that transactions clearly just in themselves, taking them one by one, may mount up in the aggregate to troubling results. Let us consider Wilt Chamberlain once more; he may stand for anyone who reaps a fortune by enjoying for a time a monopoly on some talent or device whose time has come. (Cf. L. Thurow, in *Generating Inequality*, on the random occurrence of fortune-making ventures, and the vanishing frequency with which people who succeed with such ventures succeed again with anything of the sort).[4] Every individual transaction in which a fan pays $6 or $7 to see Chamberlain play is innocent enough on both sides; hence, considering its origin, Chamberlain's aggregate success in amassing much more money than any of his fans might have to begin with does not seem unjust. On the other hand, considering what Chamberlain is now in a position to do with his greatly superior advantages, the result is troubling. He is now in a position to outbid any of his fans for scarce vital resources; in a position to drive hard bargains with any of them, much more favorable to himself than to the other party; in a position to exert power over them by hiring specialized agents to press his particular interests by whatever means are most expedient.[5] In short, he is in a position that poses dangers of unjust transactions in the future, indeed unjust departures of all kinds; and puts in jeopardy the very processes (in this case fair exchange) relied on to achieve just results.

It is true that he may be blocked from using this power nakedly. A vigorous democratic tradition in politics and a tradition in the courts of cherishing liberty may set firm limits to the power that any one person, however rich, can exert over others. Such traditions may even set some limits to the exercise of the power by a combination of rich people, on the basis of class interests. In this connection, however, one may chillingly recall that democratic and libertarian traditions may not survive hard times; Chile and Uruguay used to have respectably democratic governments and (especially Uruguay) progressive social policies, in spite of a very uneven distribution of advantages. When the crunch came, it was not the uneven distribution of advantages that gave way to liberty and democracy. Moreover, one might bear in mind the persisting anomaly that in supposedly democratic countries like Canada and the United States the features of the tax system that are progressive (in the technical sense) are largely undone by exceptions valuable to the rich and that in those countries the tax system as a whole may be regressive. There are also a lot of diffuse and miscellaneous ways in which greater advantages translate into the exertion of power: For example, the rich have much more use of the courts, and much more prospect of success in them; and can even use the courts to harass other people.

It is true, too, that notwithstanding the dangers of such increased advantages, many people, perhaps most, would consider that such things as greater security and greater bargaining power are legitimate rewards of success in the market. Can it be unjust for someone to try to earn enough in the market to protect herself thereafter from (say) the vicissitudes of employment and unemployment? I think, however, that this consideration goes no further than to allow for some limited inequality in advantages, while as things stand the advantages that Chamberlain amasses in one round confer upon him an extraordinary lead in amassing advantages in the next one. He not only has his talent to sell again; he has money to invest. The popular impression that the easiest and surest way of making a lot of money — of amassing relative advantages — is to have a lot of money to begin with is quite correct. If entrepreneurs rarely if ever have a second idea good enough, and lucky enough in timing, to make a fortune from scratch, they can readily console themselves with the thought that they don't need a second idea once they have a fortune in hand (Cf. Thurow again).[6] Advantages and with them discrepancies in power are thus cumulative.

A pretty powerful argument, which the disadvantaged are bound to find appealing and the advantaged inescapable, thus emerges for doing something to check the growth of such discrepancies, even if this means undoing aggregative results that originate in transactions just in themselves. Sooner or later, those discrepancies are going to pose intolerable dangers to the people who are on the short end of them; and all along they pose dangers of undermining to a greater or lesser degree the justice of transactions between people on either side of them (and of justice in other respects, too). I say, "Doing something." How much is to be done? How much scope is to be left for inequalities in advantages? Or to put the same question the other way round, how close an approximation to equality is to be sought? I shall begin answering this question in a moment. At this point I want to observe that the same argument which emerges for checking the growth of unequal advantages, in departures, or in a succession of departures, from the present status quo, can be turned against the distribution of advantages in the status quo itself, provided only that these are judged to be already sufficiently unequal to pose unacceptable dangers. If we can agree on how close an approximation to equality we require to reduce those dangers to an acceptable level, justice will (in our eyes) call for the present status quo to be at least as close an approximation besides calling for any future status quo to be.

How close an approximation to equality shall we require? But let us ask first in what sense are we to understand the equality to be approximated. Shall it be literal equality — the same income, property of the same value, property of the same composition — for each? Perhaps; but even more attractive, I think, is the idea of having equality far enough at least to ensure meeting basic needs, where we allow for some variation from person to person in minimum standards of provision. Some people, for example, need more food to keep going, and not merely because they are bigger or doing harder work. I assume here that agreement can be reached both on a small finite list of basic needs and on minimum standards of provision for them. Besides food, clothing, shelter, exercise, rest, companionship, sex, and recreation would figure on the list. If any items are seriously challenged, they could just be dropped, though it would be reasonable to ask first what case could be made for ascribing them as universal needs on the basis of rebuttable presumption.

Equality in meeting needs is attractive, I contend, not only because of the intuitive moral appeal of meeting needs and (consequently) relieving suffering, which is by itself as immediate as anything that comes up in ethics, and not only because of connections between needs and rights and between needs and deserts. (We may assume some condition about being willing to contribute to producing provisons, so far as so contributing is feasible and called for. Actually, free-riders, who fail to contribute while enjoying the benefits of others' contributions, stand condemned without the assumption, as participants in unjust departures other than transactions.)

Equality in meeting needs is attractive because people who apprehend not having their needs met are especially vulnerable to exercises of power by other people. Now, I suppose that people who give any weight at all to equality and to meeting needs will have grounds for insisting that the cumulation of discrepancies in advantages be checked somewhere, and that an upper bound for discrepancies must be no further out than is consistent with everyone's being assured of having her needs met. But even people who give no weight to equality at all and none to meeting needs *per se* will, because of the special vulnerability of people whose provisions for needs are put in jeopardy, have a compelling reason to agree that the upper bound must be consistent with meeting needs, and hence with equality in that respect.

Equality in that respect, however, may, in fortunate enough circumstances (which I am assuming), leave a surplus of some sort — uncommitted resources and the goods and services that can be produced with them. How shall this surplus be divided? What is at stake in dividing it is in a sense less consequential than what was at stake in making sure that people's needs are met. People are not so vulnerable to threats affecting gains or losses of items from the surplus, and in this respect the danger that greater advantages will translate into abuses of power is less for the division of the surplus. But it is still a real danger: Even people who are ready to renounce comforts in order to maintain their integrity and freedom in the face of threats have reason to fear that other people can be manipulated by comforts into cooperating with oppressors. Specialized agents could be hired on that basis. Moreover, not only are the sacrifices of comforts likely to be painful in their way to the people ready to make them; the sacrifices that they face once power is aggrandized and abused on the basis of comforts may extend into provisions for their needs. They are not going to be able to count on being free to lead a simple life of contemplation and creative activity; they must fear finding themselves locked into hard labour in the silver mines.

At this point, we might again raise the possibility of dividing things with literal, physical equality, the most convenient form of which would be an equality in wealth or money income. Many, perhaps most people would, however, think that equality could be improved on by allowing inequalities conforming to the nerve of the Difference Principle: Let there be unequal shares of the surplus left after meeting needs so long as those who get more are contributing to increasing the amounts received by those who get less. Now, there is no logical connection between conforming to this principle and reducing discrepancies in advantages to a level (span) that poses only acceptable dangers of the abuse of power. Moreover, the present inequalities in the United States and Canada, whether or not they pose acceptable dangers, are conceivably wholly in conformity with something like the Difference Principle; conceivably, they fall short of the inequalities that such a principle would license and prescribe. In the absence of a well-founded empirical theory of incentives, one can hardly tell; and a priori there is all the room that bad faith might require to defend the present distribution on this point.

I turn to the Difference Principle, however, as a further means of obtaining full currency: The less advantaged will readily agree to it; and it anticipates the most promising and the most familiar defense of unequal incomes by insisting on the test that the defense implies. Furthermore, I suspect that on experiment the present inequalities would turn out to be far greater than the Difference Principle, applied to the beyond needs surplus, licenses. Is it really plausible to suppose that Frank Sinatra, say, would sing less well and less often if he got $50,000 a year or less? (Suppose he did; we could hire another singer.) Or pay comparable to that received by General George Marshall when he directed what may have been the greatest organizational feat in history—within the space of three years training something like 10 million men in all the variety of specialities required in a modern army, equipping them, and flinging them around the globe? The claim that the top managers of the great automobile companies must have the incomes which they have if their organizational feats (such as they are) are to be forthcoming seems to me quite specious. (It is even to some extent directly belied at the moment by the behavior of Lee Iaccoca, renouncing pay and emoluments while he tries to turn Chrysler around.) The claim that they and others must, in addition, have the right to transmit the wealth that they amass to people who will not be required to do anything at all to increase the national product seems not just specious, but absurd. We can find other ways of bringing about the accumulation of capital, too.

In any case, let the matter be put to experiment: Suppose it was arranged, for example, to apply the Difference Principle to the surplus in the following sequence. (Inheritance might be attacked in coordination, simultaneously or in an overlapping sequence.) One year, the discrepancies in income would be reduced by (say) 10 percent. Then let several years elapse and at the end of them see whether either the overall amount of the surplus or the amount going to the least advantaged stratum had fallen. For this purpose—rough evidence of the effects on incentives and productivity—the mean or median of the income going to the least advantaged stratum, though not a reliable criterion for anyone choosing in the original position, would serve well enough. If, on balance, the effects were not unfavorable, a second 10 percent reduction would be carried out. Again, the effects would be observed after the lapse of several years; and, again, if the effects were not unfavorable, a further reduction would occur. And so on. When the effects began to be unfavorable, the time would come to ask whether any further reductions would be required to eliminate dangerous powers, or whether these had been incidentally to the pursuit of the Difference Principle brought down to an acceptable level.[7] At that time, too, one might consider reducing the dangers without necessarily reducing the inequalities. Some forms of distribution unequal overall to the same degree (by measures of range, standard deviation, or the Gini index) might be safer than others. Until the Difference Principle is (roughly) fulfilled, however, reducing inequalities would be the justice-favored route on which to reduce their dangers: it accords with one fully current consideration, and it is required by another.

Is this scheme, and the approach to justice involved in it, practical? I am not going to try to say whether, as things stand in Canada or the United States, it is likely to be adopted. I will make two points in defense of its practicality, first a point about the possibility of agreement, second a point about organizing the political effort.

There will be, I presume, little difficulty in getting the least advantaged to agree to the approach, once they understand what it involves and are convinced that the reaction in other quarters to trying it will not be dangerous. It is true that some confusions will have to be overcome, and some degree of acceptance of the existing discrepancy as legitimate. Jennifer Hochschild has evidence suggesting that the acceptance, which is very mixed as it stands, would disappear with the confusions.[8] People in other quarters—among the more advantaged—are in no position to argue against the approach. They are not, as I said earlier, in any position to argue against precautions establishing some limit to the growth of discrepancies in advantages. Nor are they in a position to argue against the experiment with the Difference Principle; for just their main defense of their greater advantages has been the defense of incentives to contribute, which the Difference Principle accepts. They might, alternatively, try to defend themselves by taking an intuitive stand on sacrosanct property rights. This does not seem a promising position—it brings into question their good faith in being ready to justify their disagreement by arguments; it does not (at least in Nozick's version) offer a fully current view of justice; it ignores the jeopardy in which the accumulation and concentration of advantages puts the very rights held sacrosanct. Of course, people with such advantages now may find all sorts of ways of confusing the issues and of dragging their feet; but I am not sure that one can say a priori they will reject the arguments. Jennifer Hochschild has evidence suggesting that not all of them would.[9] May they not concede the argument, but sabotage the experiment? They might simply emigrate, for one thing. I assume, however, that the experiment would be carried on at such a sedate pace that in no one move would the more advantaged be so drastically affected as to prompt large numbers of them to emigrate.

The experiment, if it is to move at a sedate pace, may take ten, twenty, even thirty years. Even ten years is a long time, one may think, for any government to pursue a large-scale goal steadily. Actually, I think there may be many examples, in policies about water supplies, or reforestation, metricization (in Canada), and the space program (in the United States), of the steady pursuit of fairly large-scale goals, even of steady pursuit through a sequence of stages laid out in advance (tentatively). None of them, it is true, concern anything so basic to the social structure as the distribution of personal advantages, or anything that poses such a challenge to present privileges, vested interests. Yet once started on the experiment, the bureaucracy might keep it going unless the experiment was countermanded; and if the government remain more or less continuously during the period in the hands of one party (as it has done in Canada), the countermanding might never effectively come. So what is mainly needed for the organized political effort to occur is for a party that is capable of coming into office and staying there to take it up. Is it politically attractive? The availability of the arguments that I have used figures somewhere in its attractions; but I expect that at the moment that is an attraction which operates indirectly. The direct attractions lie in the suggestion that nothing effective is going to be done about inflation (no incomes-policy) or productivity or morale in Canada or the United States unless each of those countries achieves a new consensus on its common enterprise, and that this consensus is not going to be forthcoming without an agreed-on approach to justice. Both countries may have to pay more attention to justice if either is going to be again the success that it used to be.[10]

Dalhousie University

NOTES

1. John Rawls, *A Theory of Justice* (Cambridge, Mass.: 1971); Robert Nozick, *Anarchy, State, and Utopia* (New York: 1974); David Gauthier, in a number of articles to be consolidated in a forthcoming book — see, for instance, "Rational Cooperation," *Nous* 8 (1974), pp. 53-65 and "Social Choice and Distributive Justice," *Philosophia* 7 (1978), pp. 239-53. In ascribing an original state of nature to Nozick, I am assuming (perhaps precariously) that he would accept as presuppositions of his doctrine some contingent facts about the past, such as that there was a time before which there were no human beings on earth.

2. Here and below I may seem to be too precipitate in finding a determinate Rectification Principle in Nozick. It is true that though he acknowledges the need for a Rectification Principle, he never tells us exactly what form it will take; and in the only passage (*op. cit.*, pp. 152-3) in which he discusses the subject at any length, he intimates that to arrive at a determinate form, a number of problems about effects on intermediary parties will have to be solved. I hypothesize that trying to solve these problems by calling for anything less than undoing all past violations of his principle of justice in acquisition and of his principle of justice in transfers would forfeit the intuitive appeal of those principles. A statute of limitations that left standing privileged positions originating in Henry VIII's dissolution of the monasteries would not work; nor would a statute that ran back to just short of 1066. See, further, the last paragraph of my Rejoinder below.

3. In a paper forthcoming in the *Pacific Philosophical Quarterly*.

4. Lester C. Thurow, *Generating Inequality* (New York: 1975), pp. 142-54.

5. Jennifer Hochschild and Michael McDonald combined to persuade me that it was somewhat anachronistic (in the United States and Canada), and hence less than fully current, to speak of people hiring "bully-boys" or "henchmen." I have substituted "specialized agents."

6. *Op. cit.*, p. 153.

7. In discussion, James Fishkin pointed out that it is possible, if the most productive people have to be offered little or no extra income as an incentive to maintain the same benefits to the least advantaged stratum, and benefits to other strata somehow disappear during the shrinkage experiment, the result of fulfilling the Difference Principle might be to reduce everyone to equal income at a low level. The main thing to say in reply is that the assumptions about incentives and leakages are empirically very improbable (which Fishkin concedes). One might also fall back on the Difference Principle in lexical form (Rawls, *op. cit.*, p. 83), reformulating it as required to safeguard Rawls's intention of not sacrificing gratuitously income to any stratum, and to make sure that in application during the experiment, GNP was no less at any stage than

at the stage before, unless the income of the least advantaged stratum was increased without gratuitous sacrifices by any stratum.

8. See her contribution to the conference, below, p. 55; also her book *What's Fair?* (Cambridge, Mass.: 1981).

9. In her book, pp. 165-81; 221-28.

10. The basic account of justice given in this paper, and the argument arising within the account for reducing inequalities in advantages, can also be found in a long essay of mine, "Justice and Injustice in Business," in Tom Regan, ed., *Just Business* (New York: Random House, 1982). There it is elaborated, even on some basic points, in ways not attempted here. Here it is commented upon, in the context of an explicit discussion of full currency, in ways not attempted there.

SOME PROBLEMS WITH "MAKING JUSTICE PRACTICAL"

James P. Sterba

Professor Braybrooke proposes to make justice practical. By this he means to require that an account of justice satisfy three tests of practicality. The first test is that an account be readily understood by ordinary literate people. Let us call this the Comprehension Test. The second test is that an account give determinate results on real world issues. Let us call this the Determinate Results Test. The third test is that an account attract steady support from ordinary people occupying both privileged and nonprivileged positions in society. Let us call this the Consensus Test.

What can we say about these three tests of practicality?.Are they good ones to apply to an account of justice? One problem is that an account of justice which "makes sense of the ideas ordinary people already have about justice" may be descriptively accurate but normatively inadequate as an account of justice. Thus the prevailing ideas about justice in a society at any one time, for example, under a religiously-based caste system, may support the status quo even when there are strong moral reasons for fundamental change. Nevertheless, when ordinary people in a society are sufficiently educated and acquainted with a wide-range of moral conceptions, the use of Braybrooke's three tests of practicality would seemingly produce quite desirable results. Let us assume, therefore, that Braybrooke's three tests are to be applied only under such favorable conditions and that such conditions obtain at least in most of today's technologically developed societies.

Employing these three tests of practicality, Braybrooke finds ample reason to reject the prevailing accounts of justice. Utilitarianism, Braybrooke claims, fails the Comprehension Test because the concept of utility is "a technical concept that has no use in ordinary life." Utilitarianism also is said to fail the Determinate Results Tests because, if determinate results are to be had, they are to be secured by the use of other notions such as need, money income, and marketbasket indices of real income. Other contemporary accounts such as those of Rawls, Nozick and Gauthier because they employ idealized hypothetical reasoning are also said to fail the Comprehension and Determinate Results Tests. Ordinary people obviously have difficulty seeing the relevance of such reasoning to real world issues, which is not too surprising when one considers that all three of these philosophers of justice have said very little about the real world implications of their views. In addition, Braybrooke claims that each of these accounts of justice runs into difficulty with the third test of practicality—The Consensus Test. On the one hand, Gauthier's and Nozick's accounts, with their virtually unqualified endorsement of pure procedural criteria, sanction actual and possible distributions of benefits that the less advantaged members of society could hardly accept as just. (And even if they were to accept the results of such pure procedures, there remains the difficult problem of how to correct for the absence of such procedures in the past.) On the other hand, Rawls' account invites rejection from the more advantaged members of society, at least for some interpretations of his difference principle.

Now there is much that I can agree with in Braybrooke's assessment of these contemporary accounts of justice. Neither utilitarianism in its usual formulations nor Rawls', Nozick's or Gauthier's accounts of justice are very practical, nor for that matter, do they claim to be. Yet faced with the failure of these accounts to be practical, we can either seek a reformulation of one or more of these views which would satisfy Braybrooke's test of practicality, or we can propose some quite different account of justice. Braybrooke clearly favors the second alternative, while I would favor the first. But before indicating my reasons for preferring this alternative, let us examine Braybrooke's own attempt to formulate an account of justice that satisfies his three tests of practicality.

Braybrooke begins by taking the present status quo as given and considers what would constitute just and unjust transactions from that starting point. Unjust transactions are evidenced by misrepresentation and non-compliance with the terms of agreement; just transactions leave the parties equally well off as judged usually, but not always, by the party's own estimates. Assuming that some such account of just and unjust transactions or procedures can be fully worked out, Braybrooke directs his attention to problems that can arise from the aggregate effects of a series of seemingly just transactions. As (pace Nozick) the Wilt Chamberlain case is said to show, wealth and power amassed from just transactions in the past can jeopardize the possiblity of just transactions in the future, and this is said to be the case even in the presence of democratic political institutions. Furthermore, Braybrooke claims that this concern for the aggregate effects of just transactions from the present status quo can extend to the status quo itself if it in turn is characterized by dangerous inequalities of wealth and power.

What then should be done to meet this danger of amassed wealth and power? As a first response, Braybrooke proposes a standard of equality with respect to meeting basic needs. Through implementing a standard of meeting basic needs, Braybrooke believes we can go some way toward counteracting the danger of amassed wealth and power. Yet even after such a standard has been implemented, Braybrooke contends that the danger from justly amassed wealth and power, although considerably blunted, still remains. To fully neutralize this danger, Braybrooke proposes utilizing a difference principle allowing for unequal shares of the surplus left after meeting basic needs provided these inequalities benefit the less advantaged. To implement this principle, Braybrooke advocates a succession of 10% reductions of advantaged differentials, followed up by evaluations of their net effects, extending over a period of 10, 20 or even 30 years.

Now although Braybrooke claims that his account of justice satisfies his three tests of practicality, I have my doubts, particularly with regard to the satisfaction of his third test — the Consensus Test. The problem as I see it is that Braybrooke's account would have trouble winning the allegiance of the more advantaged members of society, particularly those of a libertarian persuasion who are strongly committed to the legitimacy of free market transactions. For libertarians would argue that Braybrooke overestimates the dangers from unrestricted just transactions. To simply suggest the extent of disagreement here, I once heard a libertarian economist, who now has an important position in the Reagan administration, seriously contend that three or four automakers in the United States were enough to maintain a free market in automobiles. In addition, libertarians would argue that Braybrooke's difference-principle-cure would have far worse effects than the problem he seeks to remedy. Of course, Braybrooke would retort that the more advantaged members of society cannot oppose the use of the difference principle since they defend their greater advantage on the ground of the need for incentive and the difference principle takes the need for incentive into account. But, in response, libertarians would argue that free market transactions which arise from a just starting point, possibly determined by a moral equivalent of a statute of limitations in criminal law, establish property rights in addition to providing for incentive. Thus, while libertarians might concede that the difference principle takes the need for incentive into account, they would deny that the difference principle sufficiently recognizes the moral force of property rights which arise from free market transactions. Braybrooke is, of course, aware that the more advantaged might adopt this sort of defense and he seeks to dismiss it on the grounds that "it brings into question their good faith in being ready to justify their disagreement by argument." But why should we think that an appeal for the satisfaction of nonbasic needs in accord with the difference principle is based on argument while an appeal for the moral legitimacy of property rights based on free agreement and possibly some version of a statue of limitations is not based on argument? Without some further defense, I conclude, Braybrooke's account of justice would have difficulty securing the allegiance of many of the more advantaged members of society.

What then is to be done if we want an account of justice that satisfies Braybrooke's three tests of practicality? Braybrooke, I am sure, will have more to say about how to make his own account accord with these tests, particularly his Consensus Test. But I would like to suggest a different approach. First of all, I think we should take another look at those contemporary accounts of justice that Braybrooke would have us discard on grounds of practicality and see if we cannot produce more popular formulations. Actually, that shouldn't be too difficult to do since one of the reasons these acounts have maintained their currency despite their failure to come to grips with real world issues is that even in their present inadequate formulations they give expression to political ideals that are strongly held by ordinary people. What are needed, therefore, are more adequate formulations of these ideals which ordinary people can readily understand.

What then will we have? Well, definitely we will have a welfare liberal account of justice grounded alternatively in some form of a utilitarian theory or in a social contract theory or in Braybrooke's theory of needs. Just as surely, we will have a libertarian account of justice grounded in a theory of property rights or negative liberty. In addition, in order to take into account the few Michael Harringtons who still live in the United States and the many more who live in other countries we will need to formulate a socialist account of justice, grounded in a Marxist theory of society and human nature. Once we have these and possibly other political ideals formulated more adequately in ways that ordinary people can readily understand, the interesting work begins.

Will we be able to reconcile these accounts? Will we be able to show that one account is superior to the others? Possibly, but my own view is that it won't be necessary to show the superiority of one view over the others if what we want to achieve is agreement on practical issues. That is, I contend, that if a welfare liberal account of justice, a libertarian account of justice and a socialist account of justice are all correctly interpreted, they will be seen to support the same practical recommendations, which, it turns out, just happen to be those currently advocated by a welfare liberal account of justice, but which are equally defensible, it turns out, on the other accounts of justice. Thus, if I am right it won't be necessary to defeat any of the political ideals that are strongly endorsed by members of our own and other contemporary societies. We will just need to show that when these political ideals are correctly interpreted, they support the same practical recommendations. But, needless to say, the argument for this alternative way of making justice practical will have to be left to another occasion.

University of Notre Dame

A REJOINDER TO STERBA

David Braybrooke

Am I making some implicit assumptions about what ordinary people and ordinary ideas about justice are? I expect that Professor Sterba is right to suggest that I am. I should confess that I do not pretend to cover the whole range of cultural variations, and I may have to set the contented members of a caste society aside along with people from various other sorts of cultures. However, my three tests are meant to work together. I think that my third test, according to which a fully current view of justice and injustice must be agreed to by both privileged and non-privileged people, will eliminate, in most cultures anything like ours, most perverse and self-serving views. Allowing for great diversity, confusion, and conflict on the subject even so, I hypothesize that we can nevertheless find in ordinary people's views a certain core that I can seize upon to argue to agreement on limiting inequalities in distribution.

Will the agreement be forthcoming, however, cogent as the reasons may be that I marshal with that core in hand? In particular, will people agree who have a good deal to lose? I must acknowledge putting a good deal of weight on the condition appended to the third test about offering and listening to reasons. I anticipate a good deal of bad faith, manifested in a sudden onset of skepticism about statistics, in a sudden self-serving rise in standards of evidence, and in other ways. Many of these reactions will be suspect, however, and at the bottom even of complications in the data like those touched on by Christopher Morris (see the notes to his paper, below), which afford an alarming amount of room for bad faith, we might hope to match the bad faith with pertinacious suspicions. Pertinacious and well-founded though they may be, it is true, they may not suffice to finish the attack on privileges that reasoning of my sort begins. If all else fails, it may turn out that the *ultima ratio* of those currently privileged, as of Louis XIV and other kings, will be cannon.

Let us in this discussion, however, confine ourselves to reasons. Generalizing it to suit, I mean to capture in my argument all reasons that are not merely intuitive endorsements of the status quo or self-serving. I do this in two ways, in part by capturing the argument for mutual benefit with something like the Difference Principle, but more centrally by taking anything that people argue that everyone has reason to value as a feature of distribution and then showing that this—the choice of life-plans, the maintenance of certain features of social structure, the pursuit of happiness, the right to secure the means of life through hard work, fair exchange—is, when some people acquire many more advantages than others, jeopardized for the rest. Even the right to accumulate is liable to such jeopardy, and if there is a paradox involved in this fact, the paradox is not my problem. I note that David Hoekema, arriving quite independently (in the paper below) at the position that the most important argument for limiting inequalities in advantages is the argument from the dangers of unequal power, stands with me. It is not only the most important argument; it is the most general one.

Sterba's point that people with very different theories of justice may all agree on a range of practical policies is well-taken, and helps remove, in a way that Andrew Altman himself will perhaps approve, the negative impression about the chances of such agreement that might be gathered from Altman's picture (in his article below) of irreducible conflict among theories of justice taken as ensembles. I am not sure that Sterba's general prescription for arriving at agreement on practical policies is an alternative to mine. He suggests (as I understand him) adopting interpretations—the "correct" interpretations—of the rival theories now in the field such that they all support the same practical policies. I, concerned simply with one practical policy (though a rather big one) of protecting people from abuses of power resting on unequal economic advantages, let people argue for anything that they wish to secure to people, and claim that all of them must be wary of unequal advantages. So I, in effect, begin with a practical policy, and argue that each and every theory of justice has a compelling reason to incorporate the egalitarian precaution that it embodies. So far, every theory will be correctly harmonized in interpretation with every other and give the same results.

Have I gone far enough with this policy? Some might want out and out equal distribution, rather than a rough approximation; others might want a subtler application of the Difference Principle. Both these sets of people, however, may be expected to approve of the policy so far as it goes.

Have I gone too far? If libertarians could establish that substantial dangers of abuses of power fade out before the Difference Principle is fulfilled, to the extent that I would have it, roughly, fulfilled, they might have reason to hold out against fulfilling it. However, I might remark that here, unlikely as it may seem, I am working in the spirit of Robert Nozick. At the end of his chapter on distributive justice, in the absence of any good way of determining on his own principles how just or unjust the distribution is in the *status quo*, he entertains the possibility of using the Difference Principle as the principle of rectification. In effect, he offers, in embryo, an argument for redistribution that is non-egalitarian on somewhat the lines taken by Christopher Morris (in his contribution to this volume). I too am offering a non-egalitarian argument for redistribution; and in the absence of fine evidence about abuses of power, I am putting forward the Difference Principle as one compromise feature of a practical precaution. The other main feature, of course, is the condition of meeting needs, on the importance of which to justice I take the convergence of my views with Hugo Bedau's in the article below and Sterba's (explicit in his book, *The Demands of Justice*)[1] to offer substantial evidence.[2] Brian Schrag's paper shows in effect how the general concern of justice with needs works out in one specific instance; I therefore count that among the evidence, too. Confining my argument to a small list of basic needs, moreover, does not imply that I am not ready myself to join Michael McDonald, Sidney Axinn, Laurence Thomas, and Ferdinand Schoeman in their notions of what is at stake in justice besides personal needs. I think their concerns can be treated as matters of need for social beings, which people have as members of historical communities capable of furnishing goods attained only in being shared. As such, the concerns can be fitted within Bedau's wider view of the needs that are at stake in social justice.[3]

Dalhousie University

NOTES

1. Notre Dame, Indiana: 1980.

2. The convergence with Bedau's and Sterba's views is more far-reaching than will appear from my conference paper. There, as a close reading of the paper by David Banach persuaded first him and then me, the instrumental concern for meeting needs so that people will be less vulnerable to abuses of power overshadows my inclination to give needs an irreducible place in a comprehensive view of justice — such a place as would make it unjust to omit to meet people's needs even in the absence of any danger of abuses of power. I do express the inclination, but only in passing, p. 9 above. In my longer essay, "Justice and Injustice in Business," this irreducible place is clear; but in that essay I was free to ignore the difficulty of appealing to needs in this way and still, with libertarians in the field, achieving full currency.

3. Without straining for effect, I have been able, either in my paper itself or in this rejoinder, to show some convergence in themes and results with the contributions of almost every other participant in the conference. That speaks effectively for the remarkable coherence — and reciprocal instructiveness — achieved by the conference. The one paper that I have not been able to take easily into my embrace is Hardy Jones's. It is not to be inferred that I think less well of Jones's paper, or that it failed to connect up with the train of discussion at the conference. It is, in fact, an excellent example of applied philosophy; delivered at the end of the conference, it came across so effectively that it revived us all.

JUSTICE BETWEEN GENERATIONS: THE DILEMMA
OF FUTURE INTERESTS

James S. Fishkin

Our notions of individual human interests have not been refined to deal with choices where the creation of possible future people is at issue. Several recent articles have shown how this issue arises specifically for population policy and, more generally, for issues of distributive justice affecting unborn future generations. The problem, however, is more difficult than has yet been argued. Recent work on the "person-affecting" view of harm has revealed what I will argue to be only one horn of a deeper dilemma.[1] I will attempt here to sketch both horns of the dilemma and then suggest a strategy for resolving it.

A common assumption about harm is that a person can only be harmed if he is worse-off than he would otherwise have been. Parfit has called this the person-affecting notion of harm. For reasons that will be clearer later, I will call it the identity-specific notion of harm. According to this notion a given person X must be worse-off than X would otherwise have been for X to have been harmed. While in everyday life this notion of harm may operate satisfactorily, it is now well-known that where the creation of possible future people is at issue, it yields some disturbing results. In cases where most of us would clearly wish to object to a particular choice, we cannot do so within the confines of this assumption, since those who would seem, in some sense, to have been "harmed" are not harmed in the identity-specific sense. They are not worse-off than they otherwise would have been because, were it not for the choice in question, they would not have been.

To clarify the point, let me mention two versions of what have now become standard examples. At the level of individual choice let us imagine a woman with a temporary condition — a disease such as German measles or a period under required medication — such that, if she conceives a child during that period, the child is likely to suffer from serious birth defects. She faces a choice between conceiving a deformed child or waiting until sometime after the stated period and conceiving a normal child. Many of us would like to object to her not-waiting and we would like to base our objections on harms to the child. But we have no grounds for doing so, in the identity-specific sense of harm. The now familiar difficulty is that the child is not worse-off than it would otherwise have been. Another child born to the same parents, as differentiable from the first child as one sibling from another, would have existed instead.

Parallel problems for social choice can also be constructed. Imagine a developing country which must choose between a restrictive and laissez-faire population policy. If population growth is tightly restricted, general abundance and prosperity can be expected within a few generations. But if a laissez-faire policy is adhered to, the miseries of mass poverty and malnutrition from over-population will overwhelm the country within a few generations. Setting aside other issues that might arise about particular methods of restricting population growth (say, issues of liberty and equity affecting the right to procreate) most of us would say that these sharply contrasting results provide important reasons for favoring population restriction.

However, once one takes into account all of the contingencies involved in the creation of one particular population of persons rather than another, it becomes apparent that the specific people who would result from several generations of population restriction bear almost no overlap with the specific people who would result from several generations of laissez-faire. I refer the reader to some interesting calculations worked out by Thomas Schwartz on this problem.[2] This result places us in the same basic difficulty as in the birth defects case. We cannot object to the misery imposed on a future generation by the choice of a laissez-faire population because, by and large, the people who suffer as a result of the choice are not, in the relevant sense, "harmed" by it. They are not worse-off than they otherwise would have been because, except for the choice in question, they would not have been. As the generations succeed each other and the misery increases, the overlap population (between the results of laissez-faire and restriction) drops dramatically and more and more of the increasing misery cannot be counted as harm in the identity-specific or person-affecting sense.

Many people have followed Parfit's inference from this kind of case. These dramatic inadequacies of the identity-specific view of harm are taken to reveal a distinctive merit for some version of the much maligned former orthodoxy of recent years — utilitarianism. For utilitarianism permits us to take full account of the negative states experienced by the deformed child and by the over-populated, starving population, without the requirements of the identity-specific or person-affecting view of harm. We can count their disutility as disutility without having to compare their condition to how well-off they would have been under an alternative state of affairs. More generally, we can say that the assessment of interests under utilitarianism is not identity-specific; it is identity-independent. In other words, the assessment of interests is disconnected from the identities of the people experiencing those interests. It is worse to have the deformed child than to have the normal child because the disutility experienced by the deformed child is worse than the utility experienced by the normal child. Similarly it is worse to produce misery from overpopulation than to produce prosperity from population restriction because the disutility from the former is worse than the utility from the latter. There is no requirement, in making these comparisons, that the *people be the same*. Hence, by an identity-independent assessment of interests, I mean one that will support a comparison of the interests at stake in two states of affairs, without any determination of how the identities of the people under one state compare to the identities of the people under the other. An identity-independent assessment of interests is, in that sense, *anonymous*. It avoids Parfit's counter-examples by disconnecting the assessment of interests from personal identity in the states of affairs being compared.

It is important to note that utilitarianism is far from the only theory that shares this more general property. Many familiar principles permit evaluation of any two states of affairs given a listing of goods or welfare to ranked positions under the two states. In addition to utilitarianism, equality, maximin and some other, more complex principles of justice can take this form. Elsewhere, I have dubbed such principles "purely structural" since they prescribe states of affairs based on payoffs to positions without any requirements about whether the persons in those positions remain the same.[3] In this essay I will treat identity-independent theories of interests only within the confines of such structural principles (utilitarianism, equality, maximin, etc.). While it is theoretically possible that the interests might be plugged into the evaluation of states in a different way, I will make this restrictive assumption to simplify matters. All such structural principles (utilitarianism, equality, etc.) raise very interesting questions about the distribution of opportunities to acquire and maintain positions in the structure of distribution.[4] My focus here, however, is on a more dramatic defect which arises when the creation of possible future people is at issue.

I wish to argue that just as identity-specific views of harm are subject to Parfit's counter-examples, identity-independent views of harm (and of interests, more generally) are subject to an equally disturbing counter-example of a different kind. The other horn of the dilemma of future interests is defined by the "replaceability" argument, an issue raised for animals by Leslie Stephen and for abortion, infanticide and euthanasia in some recent work by Peter Singer.[5] Once the replaceability argument is juxtaposed to Parfit's work, the full dimensions of the dilemma of future interests become apparent.

Imagine a science fiction scenario along the general lines of the recent movie "Invasion of the Body Snatchers." An entire population is secretly and/or instantaneously and painlessly *replaced* by other persons, perhaps copies, who have certain desirable properties. If we are utilitarians, we might imagine the replacements to be more efficient utility maximizers. If we are proponents of some other identity-independent conception of interests (say, shares of primary goods[6]) the replacements do better along that specified dimension.

The general problem is that for any identity-independent conception of interests, so long as the abstract structure of distribution, the payoffs to positions, is at least as good under the replacement scenario, there are no grounds for objecting, at least within the confines of this kind of theory. In fact, if we are utilitarians and the replacements would increase utility, we are then obligated to kill everyone and replace them with a new population of better utility maximizers.

It is the very merit of the identity-independent principles in dealing with Parfit's counter-examples, namely, that they *disconnect* the assessment of interests from the identities of the people affected, which renders them vulnerable to this replaceability scenario. Because the interests are viewed anonymously, such theories will permit us to object to production of the deformed child or to the miseries of over-population without worrying about whether the better-off people envisioned under the alternative choice are the same people. But the same anonymous consideration of interests leads these theories to neglect the question of whether the people under the replacement scenario are the same as the people in the original population. The general dilemma, then, is that if we tie interests consistently to personal identity we face Parfit's examples, while if we disconnect interests consistently from personal identity we face the replaceability scenario.

It is worth adding that the science fiction version of the replacement scenario presents the argument only in its clearest and most dramatic form. However, on a micro-level, very similar arguments are now being employed in debates over abortion, euthanasia and infanticide. Furthermore, the sacrifice of one population for the greater welfare of future people is not a scenario limited to science fiction.[7] The replaceability argument simply permits us to define a realistic issue with greater drama and clarity, setting aside many empirical complications that would otherwise cloud the conceptual issue.

Now that we have sketched out the general dilemma, let me briefly mention two creative efforts which might appear at first glance to avoid one horn or another of this dilemma.[8] The first, formulated by Peter Singer, aspires to avoid replaceability. I will argue that it does not. The second, formulated by Jonathan Bennett seems to avoid the Parfit counter-examples. I will argue, however, that it does not.

Singer distinguishes his "preference" utilitarianism from the sensate classical version: "This other version of utilitarianism judges actions, not by their tendency to maximize pleasure or avoid pain, but by the extent to which they accord with the preferences of any beings affected by the action or its consequences."[9] From this property of preference utilitarianism Singer concludes: "Killing a person who prefers to continue living is therefore wrong, other things being equal. That the victims are not around to lament the fact that their preferences have been disregarded is irrelevant."[10]

Singer's notion is that some beings, e.g., animals, fetuses, and infants, experience utility *only* in the primitive sensate sense. Singer believes replaceability arguments still apply in their case and he explores implications of this fact for the eating of meat, and the permissibility of abortion and even infanticide. However, he believes that the applicability of utility in this second higher sense of preference utilitarianism to more developed children and adults would block replaceability scenarios applied to such persons. It is in this way that his distinction between preference and sensate utilitarianism might be taken to get us out of our dilemma (when applied, at least, to older children and adults).

I believe, however, that Singer's escape is only illusory. Preference utilitarianism is, at bottom, identity-independent and it is thus vulnerable to some versions of the replaceability scenario. This becomes apparent if one thinks carefully about what the "other things being equal" clause might mean in Singer's solution quoted above. Recall that in our science fiction scenario the replacements can *also* be imagined to have preferences in a self-conscious and reflective sense. Satisfaction of those preferences may balance out the frustration of the life plans of the previously existing population.

More specifically, if we imagine, as Singer seems to, a special disutility in an on-going life being interrupted (whether or not the person is around to regret the interruption) we might, symmetrically, imagine a special utility experienced by the replacement, e.g., utility from the miracle of his being brought into existence. The new person may experience an "existence bonus" that might very well counterbalance the disutility from the previous person's existence interruption. There is no reason, in principle, why one of these must be greater than another. The theoretical vulnerability to replaceability arguments remains.

The vulnerability is, I believe, built into the foundations of utilitarianism. It is a purely structural principle. If the aggregate (or average) utility of the replacements is at least equal to the aggregate (or average) utility of the preceding population, then there can be no *utilitarian* objection to the scenario. Counting preferences and other self-conscious aspirations within the definition of utility cannot change the calculation provided that one treats both populations (the replacers and the replaced) in the same way. The point becomes most obvious in (but is not restricted to) the special case where the "existence bonuses" precisely equal the "interruption deficits." Then the utilitarian equivalence between the old and new structure of distribution makes it evident that nothing has changed except the identities of all the particular people.

Let us now turn to a second strategy for avoiding both Parfit's problem and replaceability. It has sometimes been argued that we should only count the utilities of those who would exist were an action *not* taken. Bennett has developed one variant of this approach. While he did not direct it explicitly at Parfit's problem, its application to some of our examples is clear enough.[11] If the population planner compares the benefits of the restrictive policy with the misery experienced by those persons who would exist were that alternative *not* taken, then there is a clear case for the restrictive population policy. Furthermore, this strategy has interesting implications for replaceability. If one evaluates the replaceability scenario in terms of the persons who would exist were the replacements *not* to occur, it is clear that *they* are better off.

This strategy does not, however, offer a genuine way out of our dilemma. For it encounters the same basic difficulty as the Parfit counter-examples, namely, that it cannot be counted as a harm that someone is created to endure a miserable existence. It is vulnerable to this kind of case whenever the *others* who would exist anyway are benefited by the misery of the newly produced person. For example, imagine a population considering whether to breed a race of test-tube produced slaves. The persons who would exist were this policy *not* adopted are the present population; *they* would benefit overwhelmingly from having a race of slaves. The only ones who would suffer are precisely the ones who cannot be considered in this strategy, that is, the ones who would not exist were the policy *not* adopted. They are the ones harmed by the policy yet their misery cannot be counted by Bennett's proposal.

Let me now suggest briefly a possible way out of this basic dilemma, one more viable, I believe, than the two proposals just mentioned.

The basic dilemma only arises if we adhere, consistently, to either an identity-specific or an identity-independent assessment of interests. If we restrict ourselves to the former, we face Parfit's counter-examples. If we restrict ourselves to the latter, we have no grounds for objecting to replaceability.

There is, however, no reason why we must restrict ourselves to an evaluation of interests that conforms *entirely* to one or the other conception. There is no reason, in other words, why we cannot arrive at some notion of interests which maintains an identity-specific component that would block replaceability and an identity-independent component that would permit us to view the victims in Parfit's cases as harmed even though they are not worse-off than they would otherwise have been.

What we require is an explicitly dualistic conception of individual interests, in which one component is identity-specific and another component is identity-independent. Let me briefly mention one such conception and how it might be incorporated into a theory of justice. We might specify two distinct components in what might be called the value of human life. One component is the value, viewed *ex ante*, of a life more worth living rather than less. At least when comparing the value of a clearly miserable existence with a more benign one, we can be confident about such a comparison of possible lives. We can be confident that being born normal rather than deformed, for example, defines the developmental conditions for a life more worth living rather than less. Once created, however, we can consider a second component, the value of a life worth continuing (perhaps in the judgment of the person to whom it belongs). There is the identity-specific value to *that* person in not depriving him of his life. If we kill him he is worse-off than he would otherwise have been because he is now dead.[12]

This dualistic conception might be incorporated into a theory of justice with the following first principles:

(a) For living persons, minimize the number of deaths imposed per population.[13]

(b) For choices involving the creation of alternative possible persons, minimize the number, per population, who are born to lead clearly miserable existences.[14]

There are many controversial issues in judging *ex ante* that one life might be more worth living than another. The challenge of the Parfit counter-examples, however, was that they focussed on the *obvious* cases creating clearly miserable existences (the deformed child, the starving population) rather than lives more worth living (the normal child, the prosperous population) and the person-affecting or identity-specific notion of harm was necessarily silent about the comparison. Progress would be made by a principle that dealt with these extreme cases even if it left many subsidiary questions of population policy unsettled. That is my limited intention with this proposal.

I will assume that principle (a) would, of course, block replaceability scenarios since such scenarios would involve the killing of living persons. Principle (b) furthermore, would provide a basis for objecting to the Parfit counter-examples. Those examples are disturbing because they involve creation of persons born to clearly miserable existences (the deformed child and the starving, malnourished laissez-faire population) when lives obviously all more worth living could have been created instead (the lives of the normal child and of the prosperous restricted population). At least from these clear cases, the principle has satisfactory implications.

I do not pretend that this formula resolves, at a stroke, the many disturbing problems of justice to future possible people. I do believe, however, that it offers an example of the kind of more complex principle that deserves serious work. I also believe that if the first problem of distributive justice is admitted to be the distribution of life and death (a life worth living being the only true "primary good" in the Rawlsian sense deserving of lexical priority) then the most basic priorities of a just society can be sketched from surprisingly non-controversial assumptions. However, such an argument would require a book, not a brief article, and I will postpone it until another occasion.

Department of Political Science
Yale University

NOTES

1. See Derek Parfit "On Doing the Best for our Children" in Michael D. Bayles (ed.) *Ethics and Population* (Cambridge, Mass.: Schenkman, 1976) pp. 100-18; and Derek Parfit "Future Generations: Further Problems" *Philosophy and Public Affairs* Spring 1982 (vol. 11, no. 2) pp. 113-72. See also R. I. Sikora and Brian Barry (eds.) *Obligations to Future Generations* (Philadelphia: Temple University Press, 1978); Gregory Kavka "The Paradox of Future Individuals" in *Philosophy and Public Affairs* Spring 1982 (vol. 11, no. 2) pp. 93-112; and Jefferson McMahon "Problems of Population Theory" *Ethics* October 1981 (vol. 92, no. 1) pp. 96-127.

2. Thomas Schwartz "Obligations to Posterity" in Sikora and Barry *op. cit.*, pp. 3-13, especially p. 6.

3. See my *Tyranny and Legitimacy* (Baltimore: Johns Hopkins University Press, 1979)

especially chapter 10. I am assuming that purely structural principles specify payoffs in terms of goods or welfare in such a way as to include both harms and benefits. In such principles if death is included as a harm, it must be commensurable with the other benefits and harms measured by the theory of payoffs employed. This condition is satisfied by all the purely structural principles discussed here.

4. I discuss these issues in my forthcoming book *Justice, Equal Opportunity, and the Family* (New Haven: Yale University Press, 1983).

5. Peter Singer, *Practical Ethics* (New York: Cambridge University Press, 1979) especially chapters 4-7. See also H. L. A. Hart "Death and Utility" *The New York Review of Books* May 15, 1980 (vol. xxvii, no. 8) pp. 25-32. Stephen's original formulation of the problem is discussed by both Singer and Hart.

6. I take the notion of primary goods, of course, from John Rawls's *A Theory of Justice* (Cambridge, Mass.: Harvard University Press, 1971). Some of the interesting perplexities in applying Rawls's theory to possible future people are discussed in R. M. Hare "Rawls' Theory of Justice" in Norman Daniels (ed.) *Reading Rawls* (New York: Basic Books, 1975) pp. 81-107.

7. For applications of replaceability to abortion and infanticide see Singer *op. cit.*, pp. 122, 131-35. Joel Feinberg offers Stalin's ruthless collectivization of Soviet agriculture as an example where a population was sacrificed, putatively, for the interests of future generations. See his discussion of Koestler's novel *Darkness at Noon* in "Rawls and Intuitionism" in Daniels *op. cit.*, pp. 108-24, especially pp. 114-15.

8. It is not necessarily the case that the two poles of this dilemma must be mutually exclusive. If the side-constraint view of rights Nozick offers in *Anarchy, State and Utopia* (New York: Basic Books, 1974) is combined with the "closest continuer" theory of personal identity developed in *Philosophical Explanations* the resulting position has the novelty of being vulnerable to *both* horns of our dilemma simultaneously. First, creation of a deformed child rather than a later normal one does not cross the boundaries or violate the rights of the deformed child in the side-constraint sense. That child is not worse-off than *he* would otherwise have been. Second, if people are killed and replaced by copies, the copies can be considered the "closest continuers" of the initial population and, in that sense, the initial population is not killed at all (since they "continue"). Nozick makes this explicit in a long footnote about the *Invasion of the Body Snatchers*: "Since the old body shrivels (with the mechanism of replacement apparently allowing no overlapping time when both bodies are functioning—the second film makes this especially clear) becoming inert and without a psychology, the new body and (altered psychology) is the closest continuer at that time of the old person. It continues the person, nothing else continues the person as closely, and it continues the person closely enough to be the person; it is the person." Robert Nozick *Philosophical Explanations* (Cambridge, Mass.: Harvard University Press, 1981) p. 59.

9. Singer *op. cit.*, p. 80.

10. *Ibid.*, p. 81.

11. Bennett's proposal is that: "The question of whether action A is morally obligatory depends only upon the utilities of people who would exist if A were not performed." See Jonathan Bennett "On Maximizing Happiness" in Sikora and Barry *op. cit.*, pp. 61-73; the definition is from page 62.

12. I am restricting this inference to any life which an agent would voluntarily wish to continue. To impose death on any such person would be to make him worse-off. I will set aside some of the well-known issues about *when* he is worse-off. For some useful observations on the latter problem see Thomas Nagel "Death" in *Moral Questions* (New York: Cambridge University Press, 1979) pp. 1-10.

13. One merit of formulating this principle "per population" say, in rates of imposed death per thousand is that it avoids the well-known problem with negative utilitarian formulas (of which it is a close cousin) that it might be maximized when there are no people. One way to eliminate all pain to human beings is to eliminate all human beings. I also leave open the possibility that some caveats about the equitable sharing of risk need to be spelled out, were this principle to be serviceable. See footnote 3 above for a crucial condition of the identity-independent payoffs (in structural principles) which this formula does not satisfy.

14. By "choices involving the creation of alternative possible persons" I mean choices all of which involve the creation of some persons by the same people (or in large populations approximately the same people) at the point of departure at which the alternative choices or policies are being compared. Of course more needs to be said about criteria for a "clearly miserable existence." I am suggesting a general strategy for dealing with the Parfit counter-examples, not proposing a theory.

JUSTICE IN HARD TIMES

Michael McDonald

These are hard times ideologically: not just for those who suffer their effects — including inflation paired with unemployment, increased taxes along with diminished social services, rising arm expenditures joined to growing international tension — but also for the ideologies themselves — both (welfare-) liberalism and (neo-) conservatism. The old liberal solutions of increased government regulations and intervention are in general disrepute both with those who paid for such programmes and with their supposed beneficiaries who charge that they were misdirected acts of self-defeating paternalism which only enhanced the position of bureaucrats and social workers. Having tried conservative remedies, officially implemented in the U.S. and the U.K. but actually in place throughout the Western world via the effects of monetarism, there is the growing conviction that the cure is worse than the disease: jobs disappear, rapacious corporations line up to despoil our parks, forests, and oceans; the Mrs. Grundies are out in force in our schools, libraries, and legislatures; equal rights for women and minority groups are under increasing attack, and foreign policy is in the hands of those who long for the 'good old days' of the Cold War.

It is a situation which is likely to provoke a "plague on both your houses" attitude, particularly in the English speaking world. For, as Mill observed so percipiently nearly a century and a half ago, we in the English tradition pride ourselves on our pragmatism and are highly suspicious of intellectual movements and their attempts to provide coherent and systematic programmes of political action, just as we are suspicious of all philosophising and "doctrines générales."[1] Yet even the politics of the possible requires goals and ideals if it is to have any real direction, even the minimalist one of maintaining or ameliorating the status quo without fundamentally altering its character (which is, after all, a principal way of distinguishing our liberal and conservative movements from radical left and right wing movements).

So it is in this context (Canadian, British, American) that I want to talk about the current disaffection with both liberal and conservative ideologies. I will proceed in three steps. First, I want to provide a way of characterising and so understanding the disputes between liberals and conservatives. This will be in terms of what it is to have "a meaningful choice." I contend that liberals defend, while conservatives attack, a process of "equalization" (or transfers of resources and opportunities) to the have-nots from the haves so as to provide a floor or minimum below which none can fall. At the centre of the argument over equalization lies the issue of individual autonomy, in particular about the circumstances in which the autonomy is wrongfully or unjustly denied. This will bring me to my second point. I argue that the rival liberal and conservative notions of justice share a common, fundamental conception and ideal of rational self-sufficiency conceived as a basis for moral equality. In the last part of this paper I want to call into question this concept of moral equality and its basis of rational self-sufficiency by arguing that they and, thus, the liberal and conservative concepts of justice ignore and even undermine essential moral relationships. So I will wind up claiming that liberal and conservative notions of justice are morally inadequate. This will, I hope, raise from consideration some of the causes and cures for our current hard times with ideologies.

I. *Justice in Dispute*

Like Dworkin, I want to propose a way of understanding the deeper issues that divide liberals and conservatives.[2] My account centres on the notion of the person, in particular on the person as the subject of justice. Obviously, liberals and conservatives have conflicting ideas about what the just treatment of particular persons requires. Less obviously, they deeply disagree about the minimal conditions necessary for the "meaningful" exercise of autonomous choice. Conservatives contend that in our societies the conditions for the exercise of autonomous choice are generally met, while liberals deny this in the case of at least some persons and groups (for example, women, non-whites, inhabitants of ghettos, or the permanently unemployed). Liberals typically argue that these disadvantaged individuals find themselves in situations where they lack meaningful choices. This lack amounts to a society-wide failure to respect their autonomy, which can only be remedied by public efforts to make available significant options and the wherewithal to exercise those options. Conservatives deny both contentions: (a) that these people have been wrongfully denied anything by society; and (b) that in their present circumstances they lack meaningful options.

Let me illustrate this by considering liberal and conservative attitudes to consumer protection legislation and legislation regulating conditions of employment (hours of work, minimum wage, non-discrimination, and the like). In both cases liberals want to argue that consumers and employees in a laisser-faire situtation are so disadvantaged relative to producers and employers that they cannot make fair and just agreements with them. To remedy this, liberals propose putting government on the side of consumers and employees, e.g., by setting high standards of product liability (and relatively low standards of user liability), requiring union shops, and setting safety standards. Liberals argue that only with such measures will individuals be self-sufficient in the market-place. Thus, to take a leading case, liberals would legislate truth-in-advertising requirements to offset what they see as the autonomy-damaging powers of modern advertising. Conservatives will argue against this on the general grounds of (a) and (b) stated above, claiming in this particular instance that the consumer is free to buy the products of competitors (who will have a market inducement to advertise truthfully), sue the producer if dissatisfied with the product, and in the first instance ignore the advertising completely (by turning off their TV's). All in all, the conservative contends, the autonomy of the consumer is adequately protected by treating him as a legal equal to the producer; if the consumer fails to take advantage of that equality, it is the consumer (if anyone) who negates his own autonomy.

So while conservatives argue that having a choice of unpalatable options is not the same as being unjustly denied the choice of some option, liberals contend that it can be when the conditions of "meaningful" or "autonomous" choice are not met. Thus, liberals would "liberate" John and Mary Six-Pack (the advertising prototype of American consumers) from their bondage to Cheese-Whiz and K-tel by making available on tax-supported public media Julia Child and the Metropolitan Opera; whereas, conservatives would deny that such liberation is necessary, for John and Mary are free to purchase what goods they would like in the cultural market place. All in all then, while the liberal claims that significant segments of society are unjustly denied the opportunities for significant autonomous choices, the conservative claims that justice is done because everyone in a free market society does have their autonomy respected.

The conservative philosophy is what Henry Sidgwick labelled "political individualism" in *The Elements of Politics* (1891):

> ...that what one sane adult is legally compelled to render to others should be merely the negative service of non-interference, except so far as he has voluntarily undertaken to render positive services to others.[3]

The liberal maintains a mild form of what Sidgwick called, "political socialism" by adding to the above requirements of non-interference and contract-keeping a requirement of contributing "positively by money or services to the support of others." The liberal adds this requirement, I have argued, because he believes that such support is necessary to respect the autonomy of the disadvantaged by making available to them the means (such as education, information, income, and the like) to make meaningful choices amongst significant options. Unlike those further to the left, the liberal does not believe that this need extends to everyone in society; for the liberal denies that individual autonomy can only be realised by the radical transformation of society generally. In essence, conservatives deny both the wider more radical claim and the narrower liberal claim by asserting (i) that meaningful choices are generally and widely available, and (ii) that where they are not (e.g., drug addicts) the loss of autonomy is self-inflicted. So it is not surprising then for conservatives to emphasize the virtues of self-help, such as self-reliance, self-control, enterprise, industry, and liberty, while liberals stress the benevolent virtues, such as compassion, sympathy, and fraternity. If we picture the just social order as a competitive game, then while liberals advocate a certain amount of handicapping, conservatives can be seen as plumping for a kind of "open" competition (as in the Canadian Open).[4]

So what divides liberals from conservatives is the issue of "equalization." I borrow this term from the Canadian political context, where it has the kind of limited meaning I attribute to liberals (in which "to equalize" does *not* mean "to make equal"). Equalization payments are payments made by rich provinces (Alberta, B.C., and Ontario) to poorer provinces (the rest). The intention of these transfer payments is to provide a level of government sevices to all Canadians in all provinces sufficient to ensure full participation in Confederation. Equalization is so important in the Canadian context that it has been enshrined in the proposed new constitution (promulgated by the Queen in April, 1982). Similarly, liberals would argue generally that the well-off must make some equalization payments to the worst-off to assure the latter full or meaningful membership in the confederation of justice. This conservatives stoutly deny.

II. *Justice and Rational Self-Sufficiency*

So while liberals argue that conservatives see people generally as more self-sufficient than they really are, conservatives argue that liberals are too tender-hearted (and tender-minded) because the capacity for independent, self-sustaining activity is more fully developed than liberals realise. Now this of course makes certain "factual" disputes particularly significant, e.g., do Head Start programmes work, what are the genetic determinants of intelligence, why do members of some groups seem to do characteristically better than members of other groups? But the basic issues here are normative: are the relative differences in people's positions with respect to wealth, social status, and occupation unfair or fair?

Given the history of debate over this basic question, it may well seem that the normative (and factual) controversies are intractable and undecidable. But this is too pessimistic a view, for it ignores the important commonalities in the liberal and conservative positions. Both are grounded on a conception of justice in which the idea of persons as autonomous plays the leading role. I want to argue this even though it is clear that philosophically the concept of justice has been formulated in quite different ways, for example, as natural rights in Locke, Nozick and others, as artificial rights founded on human rationality in Hobbes and now Gauthier, and as rights constructed to account for certain moral intuitions in Kant, Rawls, and Dworkin. And, of course, there are views that do not fit easily into the above pigeon-holes, e.g., the views of Feinberg, Vlastos, Hart, and Williams. I will now try to at least outline the core of agreement.

However expressed, justice is taken explicitly or implicitly as the solution of a specific problem; call this "the problem of justice." Simply put, the problem of justice is roughly this. While people (the potential subjects of justice) have diverse plans, projects, and aims, they lack *both* intrinsic concern for the plans, projects, and aims of others *and* any common impersonal or objective scale by which to assess the value of these diverse goals. The former means that in the absence of justice people come into conflict with each other. And the latter implies that they have no person-independent ways of assessing these goals according to their worth. The only solution is then that the worth of a given end be taken to consist solely in the fact that people happen to want that end. What justice does is provide an inter-subjective (but not objective) way of resolving conflicts that arise in the pursuit of these conflicting and diverse ends.

David Gauthier put this nicely when he described justice as "the virtue that curbs the self-interest of those who are not also self-sufficient."[5] This lack of self-sufficiency is also apparent in the different states-of-nature described by Nozick and Rawls. Rawls (and Dworkin) go somewhat beyond the description of this insufficiency as solely self-interested conflict (but not in any way to which either Nozick or Gauthier would object) by describing it as a competition between diverse conceptions of the good life or life as it ought to be lived. Thus, as Rawls says in his Dewey Lectures, these are different ideas of "the Rational" or "highest-order interests."[6] In any case, there is implicit general agreement with Rawls that *pluralism* is basic to the problem justice is meant to solve.

The solution to this problem is to find "fair terms of cooperation," which Rawls labels as "the Reasonable"; such terms must embody "reciprocity and mutuality." But this, as Gauthier tells us, means that each must restrict his pursuit of his own self-interest; reciprocity here requires a shift from unconstrained to constrained maximization.[7] Now there is, as is often remarked, an element of paradox at this point or at least an apparent antinomy: namely that we each, to some extent, eschew the pursuit of our objectives to better advance those objectives, or to use Rousseauian language, we bind ourselves in order to free ourselves.

Whether or not self-interest and reciprocity can thus peacefully co-exist, or whether the former leads to the latter, the outlines of justice are clear. Each is to be granted by all the rest a meaningful guarantee of a kind of moral space (Nozick) over which he is sovereign (Feinberg); under normal circumstances (no equalization) or broadly and liberally construed (some equalization), "no trespass" or the Principle of Liberty is the rule. There must be here both agreement about what constitutes each person's sovereign territory (whether founded on natural or conventional rights or through Kantian constuctivism) and a pooling of individual resources to enforce (conservative) or provide (liberal) territorial integrity. This finds its expression in the creation of effective rights and remedies.

Because these rights and remedies belong to each and every person, justice requires the creation of a morally classless society (Vlastos) or what we might want to call, "a moral peerage" (Wolgast), in which all have the same fundamental rights and privileges.[8] To that extent, in contrast to other views like Plato's, Aristotle's, or, for that matter, Nietzsche's, justice requires full and equal citizenship for all. Whether each person or group is actually capable in the real life situations of immediately exercising the rights of that citizenship fully is, as I said in Part I, a matter of dispute between liberals and conservatives; but what is not a matter of dispute is the right to full and equal citizenship.

Basic to this picture of justice and the "problem" that gives rise to it is the notion of rational self-sufficiency or autonomy which is exercised when confronted with 'meaningful' choices.[9] If justice makes us sovereigns over our own moral territories then we must be thought of as at least minimally capable of not unwisely exercising that sovereignty. To conceive of justice as a kind of 'bargain' between those with diverse and conflicting aims, it is essential to think of the 'bargainers' as at least potentially capable of exercising a meaningful choice amongst the alternatives before them on the basis of their highest interests (as they conceive them). That is, at least three conditions must be met for rational self-sufficiency or autonomy: (i) individuals must have a rational (consistent) and realistic set of objectives or preferences; (ii) they must be capable of assessing and revising that set in the face of changed conditions in themselves and in the world; and (iii) given appropriate external circumstances they must be capable of acting on that set of preferences.[10] If these three conditions are met, then the basic requirement of justice is plausible, viz., that each is to respect the autonomy of all others. Otherwise, justice would appear to be *un jeu de folie.*

III. *Autonomy and Atomism*

I now want to return to our current ideological malaise, our deep disenchantment with both liberalism and conservatism. I think there is a very good reason for this disenchantment, viz., that the picture of rational self-sufficiency or autonomy common to both views so inadequately represents the human moral situation that both liberalism and conservatism are self-frustrating enterprises.

This can be partially illustrated by the conservative complaint that the equalization process favoured by liberals seems inherently endless: if education doesn't equalize then try social workers and welfare, if that doesn't work then job creation, and so on. Yet liberals have a strong point when they accuse conservatives of myopically ignoring the facts of racial, social, and economic inequality of the deepest sorts. Conservative nostrums of self-help here seem lamentably out of touch and even gratuitously insulting.

Neither liberals or conservatives can realise their ideals of justice because each would destroy (though in different ways: liberal through over-watering and conservatives through under-watering) the social institutions and values on which they rest. For we are not born rationally self-sufficient; we only become so over time and in relationships that cannot be that of equal to equal and certainly not that of rationally self-sufficient to rationally self-sufficient. And this is true not only of the more individualized relationship of child to parents, but also of the more socialized relationship of individuals to their culture, heritage, and language. In neither case can we picture the relationships involved as the transfer of high or low quality goods to those who are or should be treated as equals. We are not dealing here with individuals who have fixed and determinate interests on the basis of which they can judge and determine the acceptability of the merchandise we as parents, educators, and elders in society offer them. We are involved in a process of shaping or creating (within broad and ill-defined limits) would-be autonomous agents.[11] It does not help to insist that what these consumers need is more equalization to set them on a par with us. The liberal insistence on autonomy for all parodies itself here (e.g., in the assertion of equal rights for children and the ideal of a sexless society) just as the conservative portrayal of the self-made individual as the exemplar of liberty and initiative parodies itself. And what is true here of the relationship of the older to the younger is also true in many circumstances of the interrelations of adults, e.g., in doctor-patient, lawyer-client, teacher-student, and a multitude of informal relationships, rational self-sufficiency is obtained (if at all) as a kind of group or relational activity and not as the achievement of solitary individuals. If this is so, then we should picture morality as designed to solve a different problem than that considered above in Part II, viz., as I have suggested elsewhere the problem of achieving through a variety of public and private means the collective interest (cf. n.9).

Now I do not want to deny that the problem of justice presented above is not a problem for us and even for the sort of society at which I have just hinted (in terms of avoiding exploitation and stupidity). My claim is that it is not our only moral problem of any size. If we act as if it is, then I suggest we have only ourselves to blame for perpetuating our current malaise. We will create through our narrowness of vision subsequent generations that think this is the sole problem of any size. An inaccurate and misleading picture of our situation is not less powerful because of its misrepresentation, rather it threatens to perpetuate its hold on us by creating the very conditions it was meant to remedy.

Finally, I would suggest that by treating the problem of the accomodation of the interests of the rationally self-sufficient individual as the central problem of moral and political philosophy we cut ourselves off from both our own past and from a great deal of the world today, for while most of the world may envy us our wealth they do find our atomistic individualism corrosive and destructive of all they hold dear.[12]

University of Waterloo

NOTES

1. See *Mill's Ethical Writings* (New York, 1965) edited by J. B. Schneewind, especially the Introduction pp. 13-17.

2. My main difference with Dworkin is over who are the 'conservatives.' Dworkin describes

Burkean conservatives (e.g., Canadian Red Tories) when he argues that conservatives base justice on a theory of "the good for man or good of life because treating a person as an equal means treating him as a good or truly wise person would wish to be treated (p. 127). This does not really capture conservatives of the Reagan-Thatcher type or contemporary libertarians. So I am concerned with the quarrel between welfare-liberals and contemporary conservatives who would both satisfy Dworkin's description of liberalism as not espousing in their theories of justice particular views of the good life. See Ronald Dworkin, "Liberalism," in *Public and Private Morality*, Stuart Hampshire, ed. (Cambridge, 1978) pp. 113-43.

3. Henry Sidgwick, *The Elements of Politics* (London, 1902) p. 42.

4. Using the paradigm of competitive games for a just social order is basic to both the conservative and liberal concepts of justice.

5. "Three Against Justice: the Foole, the Sensible Knave and the Lydian Shepherd," *Midwest Studies in Philosophy*, forthcoming. I replied to an earlier version of this paper in an essay entitled, "On Behalf of the Foole."

6. John Rawls, *Journal of Philosophy* 77, September 1980, p. 528.

7. "Reason and Maximisation," *The Canadian Journal of Philosophy* IV, March 1975, pp. 411-35.

8. Gregory Vlastos, "Justice and Equality," in *Social Justice*, Richard Brandt, ed. (Edgewood Cliffs, 1962) pp. 31-72. Elizabeth Wolgast, *Equality and the Rights of Women* (Ithaca, 1980), Ch. 3. It should be noted that Vlastos and Wolgast are in radical disagreement over the nature of "equality."

9. Feinberg in *Social Philosophy* (Englewood Cliffs, 1973), pp. 88-94, speaks of respect for persons as a "groundless attitude" like love, citing Vlastos as well. This seems to me to distort the attitudes in both love and respect for persons. One cannot love or respect a cipher—these are intentional attitudes which need characteristic objects. In the case of the latter (the subject of this paper) I have suggested it is autonomy as rational self-sufficiency. Feinberg is right in worrying that since individuals vary in their rationality it may be impossible to insist that equal respect is a human right. I have tried to remedy this on behalf of autonomy's defender's by thinking of autonomy like citizenship: if one meets the appropriate qualification one is a citizen, no more or no less than one's compatriots. I am not, however, sympathetic to basing morality on autonomy in this or any other form, see my paper, "Autarchy and Interest," *The Australasian Journal of Philosophy* 56, August, 1978, pp. 109-25.

10. For condition (ii) see Charles Taylor's insightful paper, "Responsibility for Self," in A. O. Rorty, *The Identities of Persons*, (Berkeley, 1976) pp. 281-99. For the general conditions of autonomy see Stanley Benn's "Freedom Autonomy, and the concept of A Person," in *The Proceedings of the Aristotelean Society* 76, 1975-76, pp. 109-30. I have explicitly criticised Benn's position in the above mentioned (n.9) "Autarchy and Interest." A recent and extremely significant discussion of rationality is contained in Richard Brandt's *A Theory of the Good and the Right* (Oxford, 1979) on which I have commented in a critical notice in *Canadian Journal of Philosophy* (forthcoming).

James Fishkin (Yale) and Larry Thomas (North Carolina) pointed out that my original formulation of (iii) was too strong for it implied that autonomy required the availability of one's most preferable options, e.g., for *foie gras* accompanied by fine wine. My only aim in (iii) was to require the absence of internal obstacles like weakness of will, phobias or compulsions, so that if the subject is presented with the possibility of securing what he most wants at little or no cost, he seizes the opportunity. Thus, if he is in *Les Eyzies* in June and it is time for dinner, he will not pass up the opportunity of ordering fresh *foie gras* and *Chateau Panisseau* at the *Centennaire*.

11. Nozick's *non*-treatment of either the parent-child relation or the individual-culture relation is most revealing here. For the latter he simply treats culture and language as a kind of free good (just as air and water used to be described in classical economics). On the former he is surprisingly silent. I say 'surprisingly' for like his exemplar Locke he maintains a theory in which both the following propositions are held to be true: (i) that what one makes with one's own materials is one's property; and (ii) each person is sole proprietor of himself. See also Wolgast, p. 145. An interesting alternative approach here would be to treat culture and the like as a kind of public good which *à la* Gauthier requires enforced contributions. Rawls seems to do this in talking about education as the development of autonomy. But this, I think, raises serious difficulties. For example, why would selfish individuals want to create autonomous rivals? And, beyond that, I seriously wonder if the paradigm of justice as a contract amongst equals can be successfully maintained, for here is a clear lack of voluntariness on the part of one of the major parties as well as a lack of clear interests — a point which I have tried to make in this section of the paper.

12. This paper clearly owes a great deal to David Gauthier's extraordinary work. His paper, "The Social Contract as Ideology," *Philosophy and Public Affairs* 6, Winter 1977, pp. 130-64, makes a parallel point in its concluding sections. However, the main impetus for this particular paper comes from Elizabeth Wolgast, both from conversations with her and her most recent book (see n. 8).

THE COLLECTIVE SENSE OF EQUAL PROTECTION OF THE LAWS

Sidney Axinn

As soon as we turn to the matter of applying a legal guarantee of equal rights, we are faced with the problem presented in Choulette's well-known remark, in the novel by Anatole France, *The Red Lily*. The poor must labor, he says, "in the face of the majestic equality of the laws, which forbid rich and poor alike to sleep under the bridges, to beg in the streets, and to steal their bread. This equality is one of the benefits of the Revolution."[1] The passage is more frequently quoted than analyzed. At first it seems reasonable, if ironic, to hold that when no one is permitted to break the law, the law applies equally. This is a certain equality, *equal denial*, but it is not equally satisfactory to rich and poor. It is not equal provision.

This paper will first develop some theoretical issues involved in the matter of equal rights under law. It then will apply these issues to a brief review of some decisions of the U.S. Supreme Court that involved interpreting the equal protection clause of the Fourteenth Amendment to the U.S. Constitution.[2] Finally, it will conclude with a logical argument for the thesis that reasoning about the equal protection clause must be directed to the collective effect of a group of laws rather than to the equality of protection offered by each particular law.

I. *Bentham on the Inequality of Individual Laws*

Jeremy Bentham's *Principles of the Civil Code* is filled with discussions that are basic to many aspects of human rights, and his influence was obvious for many years after his death, in 1832. However, for the modern reader there is a certain shock effect to the way that Bentham throws one issue at us. On the matter of equal rights, he held, "If the principle were established, that all men should possess *equal rights*, by a necessary train of consequences, all legislation would be rendered impossible. The laws never cease establishing inequalities, since they cannot bestow rights upon any, without imposing obligations upon others."[3] When laws are considered one-at-a-time, we must grant his point. When I have proper possession, the law that protects my right to the property certainly denies those rights to all others. Marriage laws, as they grant rights to the couple involved, forbid just those rights to all other interested parties. Bentham insists, and one must agree, that whenever we view a particular law, we always find that it must establish some inequality. "The law cannot create rights without creating the corresponding obligations."[4]

Now it may be noted that it is just this feature of laws, the inequalities that they create, that makes them tools of social value. Bentham, in his own discussion of private property, insists that laws protecting such property are socially valuable because the alternative equality of possession was not desirable. It must also be noted that the ability to create inequalities can also be used in the opposite direction. If a situation is unsatisfactory because of a certain lack of equality, we can hope to formulate a law to change this. If we introduce a lack of equality in the opposite direction, we may compensate for the original problem. This is feasible because each law, taken by itself, does create a specific inequality. Lets take examples in each direction.

A few years ago there was no residency requirement for candidates for the Philadelphia Police or Fire Departments. Such equal consideration to residents of any area seemed undesirable to Philadelphians, and the law was amended. Only those who reside within the city limits are now eligible to apply for these positions. Because Bentham is right, a specific law does create an inequality, we can use a well-framed law to produce a desired inequality, as in the elimination of outsiders from the Philadelphia Police Academy. Nothing unusual here. Another example is the G. I. Bill of Rights which gave certain educational and other benefits to veterans alone.

There is no shortage of examples in the other direction, in the direction of increasing the amount of equality. Before publicly supported education, the ability to pay a tutor or schoolmaster limited the amount of formal education that poor children received. After the compulsory school laws, and public financing of schools, the degree of equality in formal education increased. Likewise, public swimming facilities in certain cities in the U.S.A. were once not open to blacks: new legal specifications were easy to frame, once the will to change the pattern of benefits and harm had changed.

Because Bentham is right, we can use a well-framed law to produce either more equality or less equality than existed before that law. Bentham has called our attention to the fact that each law, considered in isolation, gives an advantage to certain parties over other parties. Of course this is no limitation of law: it is the very mechanism by which we can use law to produce desired results. But this should not let us ignore the fact that if each law, taken out of its context, had to pass the test of producing exactly equal protection for the rights and ambitions of all persons, no law would be satisfactory. Strangely, the U.S. Supreme Court has sometimes argued that such a way of testing laws was both possible and proper: that a specific law in question must protect equally, all by itself.

II. *The Equal Protection Clause of the Fourteenth Amendment to the U.S. Constitution*

How has judicial reasoning met the very difficult problems in applying the magnificent equal protection clause? Somewhat inconsistently, one must say.

For most of its history, since adoption in 1868, the equal protection clause has been essentially ignored. It was often assumed to apply only to racial discrimination. However, it is framed in general terms, and its first words refer to "all persons." The clause reads, "...nor shall any state...deny to any person within its jurisdiction the equal protection of the laws." In the last twenty years we find a "newer" interpretation of the clause in which the persons protected may be any persons regardless of race (and including corporate persons). As an example of the recent kind of case, in 1975 the Supreme Court held that a state cannot require parents to support their sons until age 21, but their daughters only until age 18 (*Stanton v. Stanton*, 421 U.S. 7 (1975)). Daughters and sons must now be equally protected, financially. The court does not always treat men and women as equals. The majority once upheld a Michigan law that no female can be licensed as a bartender unless she is the wife or daughter of the male owner of a licensed establishment (*Goesaert v. Cleary*, 335 U.S. 464 (1948)). Going back still further, there was the decision, in *Bradwell v. Illinois*, 83 U.S. 130 (1873), that women do not have the right to practice law in state courts. As we know, this is no longer the last word on the right of women to practice, and to judge, the law.

A recent study reminds us of the common sense assumption that "equal protection decisions recognize that a state cannot function without classifying its citizens for various purposes and treating some differently from others."[5] But we have the court's warning that, "...the classification must be reasonable, not arbitrary, and must rest upon some ground of difference having a fair and substantial relation to the object of the legislation, so that *all persons similarly situated shall be treated alike*." (my emphasis)[6] When are circumstances similar?

If the same fee is charged to all persons who wish to buy a copy of a court transcript, exactly the same fee, are all persons treated alike? To appeal a case in Illinois, a defendant had to buy a copy of the transcript. Indigent defendants could not appeal because they could not afford the cost of the transcript. The Supreme Court held that Illinois was violating the equal protection clause by its procedure. The state did not have to arrange an appellate review; but if it did, it could not assume that defendants with widely different amounts of wealth were in similar circumstances. The court said, "there can be no equal justice where the kind of trial a man gets depends on the amount of money he has." (*Griffin v. Illinois* 351 U.S. 12 (1956) (at 19)). What determines when circumstances are similar? Sometimes the individual's wealth is a factor, and sometimes it is not. Sometimes sex is a factor and sometimes not, as we have seen. Likewise for race.

In Alabama, adultery or fornication between a white and a black was once punished more severely than between "persons of the same race and color." A Supreme Court decision held that this was not a denial of equal protection of the laws because both the black and the white got the same punishment under the statute! (*Pace v. Alabama*, 106 U.S. 583 (1882)).[7] Is adultery between a black and a white the same circumstance as adultery between members of the same color group? Perhaps a remark by Louis Henkin is appropriate, "...these days one cannot look twice in the same Constitution."[8] It should be quickly added that in *Loving v. Virginia*, 388 U.S. 1 (1967), (an ideal name for the case), the court struck down state imposed prohibitions against interracial marriages.

Are people in the same circumstances if some have lived for more than one year in the state, and others only a few months? In order to register to vote, Tennessee had a requirement of one year in state and 90 days in the county. In *Dunn v. Blumstein*, 405 U.S. 330 (1972), the court abolished Tennessee's durational residency requirement as a violation of the equal protection clause. The principle involved in deciding when people are in the same circumstances depends on the purpose of the legislation. As Chief Justice Warren once put it, "The constitutional safeguard [the equal protection clause] is offended only if the classification rests on grounds wholly irrelevant to the achievement of the State's objective. State legislatures are presumed to have acted within their constitutional powers despite the fact that, in practice, their laws result in some inequality. A statutory discrimination will not be set aside if any state of facts reasonably may be conceived to justify it." (*McCowan v. Maryland*, 366 U.S. 420, 425-26 (1961)). There are two things to be noted about Justice Warren's position.

First, the presumption that State legislatures have properly understood the constitutional limitation, and have chosen to stay within it, is quite romantic about legislative history. Things are not so. But, Warren expresses the familiar assumption that the courts must not step into a proper legislative area. An obvious criticism of this traditional cliché comes from the view that a law and its interpretation and enforcement are correlative aspects of the same piece of business. The law alone is empty without interpretation and enforcement. To paraphrase Kant: Law without enforcement is empty; enforcement without law is blind.

Second, in Justice Warren's position there is the notion that all is acceptable if the court can imagine some reasonable basis for the classification. What criteria are to be used in the rational construction of possible facts? Almost anything could be defended. Fortunately, later decisions usually have had a stricter basis than the imaginative ability, the vague speculation, of the court. The standard of not being "wholly irrelevant" can leave us with classifications that are essentially and largely irrelevant. It must be said that the Warren view appeared twenty years ago, and broader interpretations of the equal protection clause have come since that day. In *Goesaert v. Cleary*, cited, one could imagine that the purpose in denying a bartending license to most women was either 1) to keep them out of a field of traditional male employment, a male monopoly, or 2) to protect them from "social and moral problems," as some commentator put it.[9] The court chose the second construction of purpose, and upheld the law. The first assumption would have been obviously unconstitutional, even to those who might find merit in the second. The classic case of a purpose that is unacceptable is *Yick Wo v. Hopkins*, 118 U.S. 356 (1886), in which laundry licenses were refused to Chinese because of racial hostility. The idea that Chinese are to be classified as unable to operate a laundry is a perfect example of the important category of "underinclusion."

A classification contains *overinclusion* when it includes more people than it should, and contains the fault of *underinclusion* when it fails to include people who reasonably belong to it. The example of overinclusion that comes readily to mind is the restriction of people of Japanese lineage during World War II. The object was to find a classification that included just those who were a military threat to the nation, but the law classified all Japanese as such. Among the suspicions that one brings to this is the notion that perhaps the relocation law was intended to eliminate competition from Japanese businesses and farms, rather than merely protect from sabotage. Recent decisions awarding compensation to those Japanese who were restricted to prison camps would have to be considered, if racial cases were the central question in this paper.

In addition to the categories of over and under-inclusion, constitutional law has made serious use of the vocabulary of "suspect" classifications. A classification by race is automatically held to be suspect, and given careful review. Limitations on the ability to vote have also been taken to be suspect, for obvious reasons, as have restrictions on aliens. The court has thrown out laws that restricted certain aliens (those ineligible for citizenship) from receiving commercial fishing licenses (*Takahashi v. Fish and Game Commission*, 334 U.S. 410 (1948)), and from the right to own real property (*Fuji v. State* 38 Cal. 2nd 718, 242P. 2d 617 (1952)).

In addition to a) over and under-inclusion, and b) the suspect categories, there is c) the matter of "fundamental interests." The court has given special consideration to classifications that concern voting (as mentioned), procreation, and rights that involve criminal procedures and education. There does not seem to be any clear way of characterizing this view of fundamental interests, beyond the *ad hoc* remarks in each case. Decisions in even these three kinds of cases are far from predictable, because of corresponding notions such as "benign racial classification," used to overcome prior discrimination. However, a matter involving these so-called fundamental interests will trigger special attention by the court.

We started with the question, "When are circumstances similar?" After a brief notice of an assortment of cases, what can be said in response to our question? To make the relevant circumstances similar, we have three principles. One, there must be neither over nor underinclusion in the class. Two, the suspect categories must be given very careful attention to avoid using a superficial purpose to conceal the actual purpose. Three, fundamental interests must take precedence over superficial similarities. Each of these principles, or practices, has a primitive term that needs precision. These key terms, of course, are "fundamental," "suspect," and "over and underinclusion." Underlying the entire matter is the individualism in the application of the equal protection clause. Let us turn to this.

III. *Logic and Legal Nominalism*

As a survey article puts it, "The Supreme Court has declared that the equal protection clause confers individual rather than group rights to equality...equality of treatment must be measured as between individuals. Individuals should not be treated differently unless there is a relevant distinction between them, and one's race is ordinarily irrelevant to any legitimate public purpose."[10]

On this matter of application to individuals alone, Professor Owen M. Fiss (Yale Law School) has given a very impressive analysis, holding that the law should be directed to discrimination against groups. This, he says, would "take a fuller account of social reality."[11] He proposes this as a "mediating principle" in applying the equal protection clause. Presumably it would be available in addition to the principle of discrimination against an individual.

This notion of protecting a group rather than merely considering the individual has its attractions: these are the attractions of a wholesale rather than a retail way of managing. However, the healthy nominalism implicit in the Bill of Rights, and in Bentham's work, makes me suspicious of putting more than nominal (!) confidence in an abstract entity like a group. Unless, of course, the group term be considered merely as an abbreviation for the list of its members (to add a bit of the nominalist catechism). To protect groups *qua* groups in preference to individuals is certainly undesirable. Therefore, while I urge that serious attention be given to the paper by Professor Fiss, I shall argue for what I find to be a more powerful alternative that is free of the distasteful aspects of the group formulation. The focus here will be on *the laws as a group, not on the people as a group.*

IV. *A Simple Point of Logic: The Fallacy of Composition*

The technique for testing a law to see if it offers equal protection to the individuals concerned has been to ask, "Does this law classify in a discriminatory fashion?" Understandable, certainly. However, the Equal Protection Clause is phrased in terms of the protection of "the laws," plural. Is there a difference between the distributive and the collective senses of "the equal protection of the laws?" The Fallacies of Composition and Division force us to acknowledge that a collection of laws *may* have properties that are different from the properties of the laws considered one-at-a-time. The Fallacy of Composition is the fallacy of assuming that if each one of a group of individuals lacks a certain property, the group cannot have the property. In another variation, if each one of a group of individuals possesses a certain property, the group must also possess that property. Example: if no one of the individuals in a certain room weighs more than two hundred pounds, the group cannot weigh more than 200 pounds... how could a group have a property that is not possessed by its members? Clearly an elementary fallacy. The logic of the fallacy of composition holds generally, and that means that it may affect the relation between a set of laws considered distributively (one-at-a-time), and the set considered collectively.

Even if each one of a set of laws appears to give equal protection to the people concerned, the set of laws as a group might not give equal protection. We cannot know the group effect merely by being satisfied with the laws considered individually. For all its attention to classifications that are suspect, benign, and unfairly inclusive, our constitutional law has simply not given much weight to this feature of the clause. *The laws as a collection must not deny equal protection.* To simply test laws individually, and ignore the effect of the set of laws in an area, is to make a mistake in logic and sometimes a mess socially.

A less formal way to put the point is to insist that nothing has meaning out of context...and this holds for laws. As Bentham has argued, if each law, taken out of its context had to pass the test of producing exactly equal protection for all persons, no law would be satisfactory. However, laws are effectively syncategorematic. Their meaning, purpose, and basis for praise or condemnation depends on the social context. To determine whether a law protects or damages someone's interest, we must consider the situation to which the law applies. The entire set of circumstances may not be relevant, but some part of them must be. These circumstances always include the existing laws in the area that are relevant to the situation, as well as the impact of the new law under consideration. It is the combination of the new law with the whole collection of existing laws and circumstances that exerts protection or harm.

Suppose the question arises of whether a proposed new law would produce more equality or less equality, along some dimension. We would have to make some assumption about the situation before the new law, and the expected situation after the new law takes effect. An evaluation of a new or an old law is an estimation of its effect in combination with all the other existing legal and other relevant factors. The "protection" or benefit of the laws can be equal if and only if we are considering and concerned with the cumulative effects of the whole package of laws that apply to the particular situation.

V. *Application to the Bakke Case*

How do these two matters apply to the Bakke case, the question of a "special admissions program?" Can special admissions programs be labeled unconstitutional on the basis that they deny equal protection of the laws to someone not qualified as "special?" As argued above, it is the cumulative effect of all the laws, and not just one of them, that must provide "equal protection." Therefore, the question in *Bakke* was not merely, "Does the California law involved in financing the special admissions program at the Medical School (of the University of California at Davis) protect Mr. Bakke as much as it protects a random one of the sixteen students admitted under the program?" Of course any one law or its application will provide something to someone and take something away from others. Our serious question, to be considered under the guidance of the equal protection clause, is: "*Do all the laws relevant to medical education* give all the citizens a more nearly equal amount of protection with or without the special admissions program?" Of course, medical education requires attendance at elementary, junior, and senior high schools, and an undergraduate college. Included among the laws involved in education are those that determine the basis and the amount of tax money collected and actually spent in the different school districts. Each of these laws must certainly create some inequality: we must apply our attention and best efforts to *the effect of the whole combination of laws on the candidates for admission to a particular state run school.*

How wide a scope must be considered in weighing the effect of some particular law? The matter of "area of discourse" has been well-developed in 5th amendment cases of the early fifties, and it also arises here. This matter of scope is certainly a proper question for the court in a particular challenge, and it would have to be at issue and addressed by counsel for each side. In the defense of the special admissions program at Davis Medical School, I should expect that all laws involved in the educational preparation of the candidates for admission would be considered relevant to the matter of equal protection in that case. Pertinent material would include the tax resources made available to the schools attended by the minority and by the majority candidates. If the whole combination of relevant laws do provide essentially equal protection to the educational hopes and opportunities of both majority and minority group candidates, then special admissions programs would be invalid under the 14th Amendment. This is the consequence of understanding the equal protection clause to refer to the laws collectively not distributively. Following Bentham's analysis, this is the only way such a clause can be understood.

Civil liberties and minority aspirations for some preferential treatment are not at risk in a strict construction of the 14th Amendment. They are massively supported. It is the cumulative effect of all the laws, and of the acts of the executive and judicial branches of government, that are to pass the requirement of "equal protection of the laws." Otherwise we are left with the obvious unfairness described in the remark by Choulette in the Anatole France novel, with which this paper opened. As Bentham knew,[12] laws simultaneously deny and provide. But equal protection of persons by laws requires more than equal denial...it requires equal provision.[13] We locate the results of the denials and provisions only when we measure the collective or cumulative effects of the combination of laws. As argued above, to consider the laws just one-at-a-time is to be guilty of the Fallacy of Composition.[14]

Temple University

NOTES

1. Anatole France, *The Red Lily*, The Modern Library, Boni and Liveright, Inc. New York, p. 75.

2. The Fourteenth Amendment was ratified and became law on July 28, 1868. It was one of the post-Civil War amendments that forbade slavery and its legal consequences, among other things. The first section reads:

> 1. All persons born or naturalized in the United States and subject to the jurisdiction thereof, are citizens of the United States and of the State wherein they reside. No State shall make or enforce any law which shall abridge the privileges or immunities of citizens of the United States; nor shall any State deprive any person of life, liberty, or property without due process of law, nor deny to any person within its jurisdiction the equal protection of the laws.

3. *Principles of the Civil Code*, Bowring edition of Bentham's *Works*, Vol. I, pp. 312-13. Quoted as reprinted in D. O. Wagner, *Social Reformers*, Macmillan, New York, 1959, pp. 50-51.

4. Wagner, cited, p. 49.

5. *Harvard Law Rev.* Vol. 82, p. 1076.

6. *F. S. Royster Guano v. Virginia*, 253 U.S. 412, 415 (1920). Cited in *Har. L. R.* 20, p. 1065.

7. The quotation is taken from the discussion in H. Taylor, *Due Process of Law and the Equal Protection of the Laws*, Chicago, Callaghan and Co. 1917, p. 603.

8. In a book review in *Harvard Law Review*, Vol. 82, pp. 1194-95.

9. In *Harvard Law Review*, Vol. 82, p. 1097.

10. *Ibid.*, pp. 1111-12.

11. Owen M. Fiss, "Groups and the Equal Protection Clause," *Philosophy and Public Affairs*, Vol. 5, No. 2, Winter 1976, pp. 107-77. Quotation, p. 108.

12. Some of the histories say that the equal protection clause is apparently an invention of the U.S. Congress. It does not seem to have a clear history in common law. For some commentators the term "equal protection" is hard to understand in terms of the framers intention because, "the term had no significant history prior to incorporation in the fourteenth amendment." (*Harvard L. Rev.*, Vol. 82, p. 1068.) The clause was drafted by John A. Bingham (R. Ohio), first in the form of a positive assertion of the power of Congress, and then, to har-

monize with the form and style of the Fifth Amendment, to a negative injunction on State power. This discussion is in Alan P. Grimes, *Democracy and the Amendments to the Constitution*, Lexington Books, D. C. Heath and Co., Lexington, Mass. 1978, p. 47.

The commentators mentioned above may have overlooked the brief but interesting analysis of the matter that Bentham gives in his *Principles of the Civil Code*, cited. He concludes that, "...all things considered, the protection of the laws contributes as much to the happiness of the cottage, as to the security of the palace." (Wagner, cited, p. 52)

13. On the logic of the relations between denial and affirmation, see my "Fallacy of the Single Risk," *Philosophy of Science*, Vol. 33, Nos. 1-2, March 1966, pp. 154-62.

14. David A. J. Richards, in his *The Moral Criticism of Law*, (Dickenson Publishing Co., Encino, California, 1977), offers what he calls "the moral theory of the equal protection clause" (p. 153). He applies this to school financing cases by developing a very impressive notion called "the concept of opportunity." I certainly agree with his conclusions, and his comments about the morality of the several decisions on school financing. However, I think that the consideration of the collective effect of the laws in a particular area would put these matters on a clearer logical as well as moral basis.

JUSTICE, THE POOR AND THE REDISTRIBUTION OF WEALTH

Jennifer Hochschild

"Why," as Werner Sombart asked, "is there no socialism in the United States?"[1] More precisely, why do the American poor not seek the downward redistribution of wealth? The United States does not now have, and seldom ever has had, a political movement among the poor seeking greater economic equality. The fact that such a political movement could succeed constitutionally makes its absence even more startling. Since most of the population have less than an average amount of wealth — the median level of holdings is below the mean[2] — more people would benefit than would lose from downward redistribution. And yet never has the poorer majority of the population, not to speak of the poorest minority, sought seriously to vote itself out of its economic disadvantage.

Obviously, a complete answer to the question of "Why no socialism?" would involve institutional, historical, biographical, and economic analyses, among others. Here I address one facet of this broad topic — the disparity between support by the American poor for political action to mitigate the effects of poverty and the absence of support by the same people for political action directly to end poverty by redistribution. I first show this disparity, and then argue that its cause lies in the difference between Americans' norms of economic justice and of political justice. I develop a typology of norms of distributive justice, and use intensive interview data to show how poor Americans accept economic differentiation while seeking greater political equalization. Finally, I address the political consequences and context of this disjunction between views of economic and political fairness.

The Distribution of Income and Wealth

Despite the growth of the welfare state, the distribution of income between rich and poor has not changed significantly in the United States since the Depression. In 1935, the poorest 20% of the population received 4.1% of the nation's income; in 1977, the poorest quintile received 4.3%. The second quintile has gained only trivially — from 9.2% in 1935 to 10.3% in 1977. The third quintile has gained a little more, going from 14.1% to

16.9% in those forty years. The fourth quintile has gained still more, from 20.9% to 24.7%. The richest 20% has lost some of its share, going from 51.7% to 43.8% of the nation's income. The wealthiest 5% within the top quintile has lost even more, moving from 26.5% in 1935 to 16.6% in 1977.[3] Thus the poor are staying poor, the middle and especially upper-middle strata are gaining income, and the wealthy and especially the very wealthy are losing income. "Trickle-down" policies have seeped down only through the upper half of the citizenry.

Wealth is much more unevenly distributed. In 1970, the most recent year for which we have even partial data, the poorest quarter of the population held only 8% of the nation's wealth; the wealthiest 3% held 29% of the nation's wealth.[4] Note finally that income is more unequally distributed in the United States than in eight of nine advanced industrial non-Communist nations (we have no comparative data on wealth).[5]

Attitudes Toward Redistributive and Social Policies

Nevertheless, most of the poor do not seek to have the government change their circumstances. In 1939, only 24% of the poorest thought the federal government should confiscate unneeded personal wealth to "use it for the public good."[6] In 1969, only 14% of the poorest agreed that "every family in this country should receive the same income."[7] The poor do, however, consistently support government programs to aid the poor. With very few exceptions, well over 50% of those with grade or high school education sought more federal spending on education, low-cost housing, medical care, and welfare aid during the 1960's and 1970's.[8] The poor are not simply indiscriminate big spenders; many fewer than half of those with grade or high school education (and sometimes as few as 6%) supported more federal spending on defense, foreign aid, and space exploration during the same period.[9] The poor consistently support government compensation for unemployment, national health insurance, the creation of more public service jobs, and more job training programs.[10] Why do the poor and near-poor ask the federal government to alleviate the effects of poverty but not directly to attack poverty itself?

Norms of Distributive Justice and Domains of Life

To answer this question, we need to explore norms of distributive justice. I argue that beliefs about justice can be arrayed along a continuum, with end-points of a principle of equality and a principle of differentiation. The *principle of equality* is a prima facie assumption that all people may legitimately make the same claim on social resources, despite differences in race, sex, ancestry, prior holdings, talents, achievement, rules of the game, or luck. The *principle of differentiation* is a prima facie assumption that differences in race, or sex, or ancestry, and so on create legitimately different claims on social resources. The six norms range from a belief in pure equality to a belief in pure differentiation, as shown in Figure 1 below:

Figure 1. Norms of Distributive Justice.

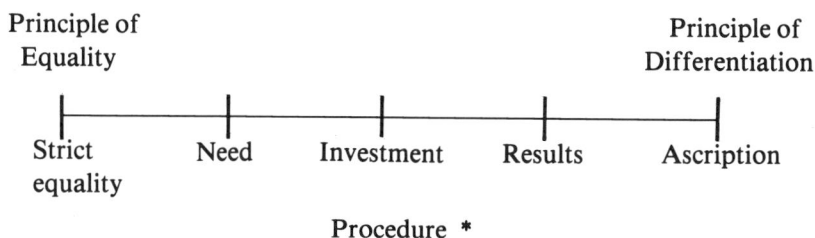

Principle of Equality				Principle of Differentiation
Strict equality	Need	Investment	Results	Ascription

Procedure *

*The location of the norm of procedure along the continuum depends on the procedure used.

I define the norms as follows:

(1) *Strict Equality*: All community members deserve equal amounts of the good being divided. Alternatively, members should sacrifice equally when necessary.

(2) *Need*: All needs of community members deserve equal satisfaction. Alternatively, members should sacrifice equal amounts of satisfaction when necessary.

(3) *Investment*: Community members deserve rewards in proportion to what they put into the community. This norm forms the midpoint of the continuum. It is egalitarian if the investment is equally available to all and always achievable (for example, effort or virtue). It is differentiating if the investment is not equally available to all and need not be renewed once obtained (for example, education or training).

(4) *Results*: Community members desedrve rewards in proportion to their productivity or social contribution, usually but not necessarily measured by market value. This is the first clearly differentiating norm.

(5) *Ascription*: Community members deserve rewards according to relevant ascriptive traits such as age, sex, race, class, religion, or ethnicity.

(6) *Procedure*: Community members deserve rewards according to the results of specified processes such as free consent, random rules, the

market, or social Darwinism. This norm does not seek patterned results; therefore, without further information, it cannot be placed on the continuum. The choice of a procedure, however, often depends on the basic principle being followed. Majority rule and random rules assume initial equality of persons; social Darwinism and a free market assume differences.

To make these rules of fairness relevant to my original question of why the poor want the polity to relieve poverty but not to end it, I need one more set of concepts. These are the domains of life to which norms of justice are applied. Three are relevant here: 1) the *socializing domain* — the arena of home, family, school, friends, and neighborhood; 2) the *economic domain* — the arena of the workplace, marketplace, and social structure; and 3) the *political domain* — the arena of tax and social policies, political rights and authority, and visions of utopia.

Figure 2. The Three-Part Pattern of Beliefs about Distributive Justice.

	Domains of Life		
	Socializing	Economic	Political

Principle of
Equality
	Norms of:
	Strict
	  equality
			Norms of:
			Strict
			  equality

Principles of Distri- butive Justice	Need Investment Procedure	Norms of: Investment Results	Need Investment Procedure
Principle of Differentiation		Ascription Procedure	

* The area encompassed by the political domain overlaps that of the economic domain considerably, in order to show graphically that people often mix egalitarian and differentiating norms in their political judgments. See Jennifer L. Hochschild, *What's Fair? American Beliefs about Distributive Justice* (Cambridge, Mass.: Harvard University Press, 1981), chapter 6.

My basic premise is that people apply different distributive norms to different domains of life, and that they largely derive their views of redistribution and other policies from their underlying conceptions of what is fair in a particular domain of life.[11] More precisely, people generally use a principle of equality, and thus egalitarian norms, in the socializing domain; they use a principle of differentiation, and thus differentiating norms, in the economic domain; and they return to a principle of equality, and thus to egalitarian norms, in the political domain.

Thus poor Americans begin from an assumption that they are equal to all others in their home life, school, community, political rights, and policy interests. However, they begin from an assumption that they are either better or worse than—at any rate, not necessarily equal to—all others in their economic and social worth. Justice, then, requires differentiation in economic matters but equality in personal and political matters; justice is not a matter of finding the right rule for all occasions.[12] This pattern is illustrated in Figure 2 above.

Distributive Norms of the Poor

The principles of equality and differentiation, the six norms of distributive justice, and the three domains of life are all conceptual. The three-part pattern of support for socializing domain equality, economic differentiation, and political equality is empirical; it emerged out of intensive interviews with a small (16), randomly-selected sample of white working adults with incomes below $10,000 in 1975.

I have room here for only the briefest illustration of this empirical work. Consider two respondents. Maria is 55, works as a cleaning woman, and earns $7000 a year to support seven people. Eugene is 68, a salesman, earns about $10,000 a year and has no savings. Eugene and his wife Vivian use a norm of strict equality in the home:

Eugene: We cook together, clean the dishes together, wash the floors, do the windows together. We just, it's a natural thing. We didn't say, "This is your job and that's my job." We just, it had to be done—just both done it. Right, Vivian?

Vivian: Even our money situation. We don't say, "This is yours, this is mine." It's just ours. Our work is ours, and our money is ours.

Maria, who is poorer, concentrates on the norm of need. Discussing scholarships to the local vocational high school, she expostulates: "It's the ones that *had* money got it [the scholarship]. It wasn't fair. A doctor's son got it, or a businessman that's got the money, their kids get the scholarships. You wouldn't hear anyone that needs, really *needed* it, got it." She concludes bitterly, "You have to have money, otherwise you don't get it."

But neither Eugene nor Maria think that incomes should be divided equally or according to need. Maria uses a norm of results to justify her employers' wealth: "They worked for it, why not? You work for it, it's fair... Well, if you're making less than I am or I'm making more than you, why not? If I got a good education and I'm doing a different job, entirely different job, and a harder job, I deserve more. If you're not doing anything, just sitting around doing, you know something light. But if you deserve it, you deserve it. I don't believe in this equal, all equal." Even those who gain riches through inheritance, not productivity, should be able to keep their money. "If their parents were wealthy and they inherited it, good, fine. Sure, it's fair. Good luck to 'em."

Eugene uses a differentiating procedural norm of unbridled competition to explain and justify great wealth. The wealthy "outsmarted other rich men, and other smart men, to get that money. They knew how to maneuver their money. That's how you get the big money, by manipulating, gyping somebody. Above the law or within the law." Despite his personal egalitarianism, Eugene views the Hobbesian war of all against all as a perfectly fair and legitimate form of activity in the economic domain: "It's their money—do as they please. If I was rich, I wouldn't want anybody telling me what to do with my money. Do what *I* want with it. I earned it, I maneuvered, I stole it, I did everything to get it. Well, if a guy got rich, just robbed banks—and he had people working for him just robbing 'em banks of all that money, that's *his*. He took all these chances. It belongs to him—nobody got to tell *him* what to do with it." He has no illusions about equality of opportunity: "Because you're poor, you don't have the chance. And the rich man—they have the better opportunities. Money, money buys almost everything. Money could buy an education, money's at the top of the list all the time." Clearly, both use a principle of differentiation to evaluate what they see as purely economic issues.

And yet, when Eugene and Maria talk about the political domain they return to a principle of equality and norms of strict equality and need. However they, like the other respondents whom they represent here, do not shift from economic differentiation to political equality as abruptly as they had shifted from equality in the socializing domain to economic differentiation. Instead, as the issue discussed changes from political manipulation of material goods (e.g., welfare, tax policy) to purely political matters (e.g., rights, authority), they move from somewhat differentiating to strongly egalitarian norms.

Thus Maria wants the government both to protect private property and to limit the harm that property rights can inflict on the poor. For example, neighborhoods may not expropriate price-gouging stores, but the government should "force storeowners to lower the price." She is more clearly egalitarian about taxes. The federal government, says Maria, should stop "tak[ing] so much taxes out. Take it from the other people that have it, the richer people. They get away with it, without paying the taxes. And *we* have to pay the taxes. We pay more." People making less than $15,000 should pay no taxes, people making $15,000 to $40,000 "should pay a little more, if they're making more," and "if they're making a *whole* lot, why not take more from them? Then the one that makes the less shouldn't pay as much." Asked what she would do if she could control the use of tax revenues, she answers defiantly, "I'll tell you the truth, share it. Yeah, sure, why not? Share it with the people! Don't take out so much taxes. Take it from the rich, like I say, give it to the poor. That's how I feel about it. I'm honest, right?"

Maria is more confused than anything else about the nature of political rights, power, and representation, but even her disjointed views on these matters are basically egalitarian. She is angry, for example, that politicians bail out failing industries—"They wouldn't help the poor, why should they help the rich?"—and that the legal system penalizes the poor who cannot hire expensive lawyers—"Whether they have money or not, they should get the same thing like we would get if we went to court."

Eugene is more concerned about governmental response to the needs of the poor and middle class than about equality of sacrifice or rights. He too wants property rights to be protected: even the claim of eminent domain, which most respondents grudgingly accept, is "wrong. He bought that property, it's *his* property. I don't care if they want to put a hospital there. Go pick some other spot. Start a new town. Don't take my land." And yet, he has a long list of social welfare policies that he would like the government to enact—so many, in fact, that "years ago, when anybody talked like this, they were Communist." The government "should have a program where they get enough to eat, and that they could be able to get a doctor. There's not enough doctors and there's not enough medication. That's the suffering. And not enough food for poor people. They give them the stamps—people gotta have money to buy stamps. These real poor people, they can't even buy stamps." Furthermore, he continues, "they don't have enough schools, they don't have enough playgrounds, they haven't got enough projects, the government. Haven't got enough trade schools," or convalescent homes, low-cost housing, public transportation, and so on. But if government would tax the rich properly, and if it would then "share it [tax revenues] a little bit more to the people," there would be enough to enact social policies to aid the needy and help to equalize all citizens' well-being.

Eugene is unambiguously egalitarian in evaluating purely political rights, and just as discouraged as Maria about their enactment. We have "justice [only] for the rich, not for everybody. There's supposed to be justice for all, [but] a lot of the laws were made for certain people." Special treatment for the rich or other categories offend his belief in our innate equality: "I meet all kinds of people. They may have a better position, [but] they're not better than me. They're all human. We are all born equal; the Lord gave us two hands, two feet, and a brain if you will use it."

Up to this point, I have illustrated Figure 2, showing that the poor see justice as egalitarian in personal and purely political contexts but as differentiating in an economic context. So long as they can keep domains of life compartmentalized in their minds and daily behavior, they, and the polity, can live comfortably with this disjunction in beliefs about fairness. But the question of redistribution of wealth creates a confrontation between the economic and political domains. When citizens view redistribution as an economic question—i.e., "How much income should people receive?" —they argue from a principle of differentiation and oppose it. When they view it as a political question—i.e., "How much should the government help to improve the lives of the poor?"—they sometimes argue from a principle of equality and favor it. The *political* redistribution of *economic* holdings, by definition, straddles two domains and forces people to confront the disjunctions in their beliefs about distributive justice. If there is no political payoff for trying to resolve this muddle between conflicting norms, since the polity has never seriously considered redistribution, and if its resolution would require a great deal of energy and mental strain, the most rational thing to do is to ignore it. Thus most people refuse to consider the possibility of—or "oppose"—redistribution even though it would materially benefit them.

Let me, once again, illustrate these propositions through Maria and Eugene. Maria supports a minimum income for all, but first emphatically rejects a ceiling on incomes because "if you're a doctor, you deserve more. I'm only cleaning house." Later, however, she is uncertain: "I don't know. I never really looked into that. Close to the same would be a good idea. No, I don't know, I don't really go for that. If you're working hard for something, and you're making a little more money, I believe in that." Still later, "If we all made good money, it would be great." Her vision of the best possible future for the country is "that we could all live normally, and not have to worry about money or anything. And have a good life, you know, not have to struggle like this." She continues this vacillation throughout our conversations.

Eugene too is torn between economic differentiation and political equalization. Placing a ceiling on incomes is unacceptable: the government "can't stop a man from making money, 'cause free enterprise means that you gotta keep a man going and keep his ambition going." Going a step further, to equalize incomes, is impossible. With equal holdings, we would "turn out to be a bunch of cannibals. We'd be stealing from each other, killing each other, trying to take away from the ones that *are* satisfied. It can't be." Eugene reinforces his vision of a war of all against all with an ascriptive argument about the need for hierarchy:

> Well, it's human nature. There has to be all classes of people. Doesn't sound right, but that's the way it's gotta be. Because it'd be a hell of a world to live in, if we didn't have some rich and some poor. You gotta have all classes. Who'd mow your lawn then? Who'd do your housework? Who'd go picking up the garbage? You gotta have people with money that you have to look up to and do work for them. We don't, most of the people don't like rich people; that's what's gotta be. You don't just wave your wand and change things. It'll always be that way.

But still, Eugene objects to price-gouging by storekeepers, tax evasion by the rich, and exploitation by landlords, doctors, and lawyers. In fact, "I think anybody could live with $50,000 very comfortably. Anybody that makes more money than they'll ever be able to spend don't deserve that kind of money. They're only taking most of it from the average working man."

Thus the idea of having the government equalize incomes throws both respondents into confusion. It forces them to face the fact that their views of economic justice contradict their views of political justice. Maria has no idea about how even to begin to reconcile her views or to reform the world that has hurt her so much: "I only hope things get better, instead of what they are now. Change the government—no, I shouldn't say that, huh? I don't even know what you'd have to do to change it. Get all these men out that (pause) then put the new ones in? I wonder if it would make a difference. Maybe it wouldn't." She cannot imagine a worse life than the one she is living—"The worst? (pause) Can't even think of anything. What would be worse than what I'm now? This, this *is* the worst for me. The way things are now." And she has no hopes for improvement: "If the middle class people and the poor, they got together, maybe there's something they could do. Actually, you don't see anything like that happening though. Nope, that'll never happen" unless there is a "miracle."

Eugene refuses to despair over the contradictions within his beliefs and over the evils in the world around him. He searches for a way to reconcile his irreconcilable views of justice. The government should let a businessman or landlord "make all he wants, but *tax* him. He can keep making millions, he can be a billionaire—let him pay tax on it." Similarly, the government should limit "what they [doctors] should charge. Not what they could *earn*, but what they should *charge*. Let the man earn, but not charge the working man or anybody. Because when they charge people, that goes for the one that *can* afford it and the one that *can't* afford it." But even he recognizes the faulty logic in his arguments, and he retreats into a dismissal of the problem of equality altogether: "No, it doesn't make me mad. I'm pretty open-minded about all these kinds of things. It's no good to do that. I know I don't *like* it, but I don't get mad. Otherwise I would be in the nuthouse. I make the best of a bad bargain. I make myself satisfied with what I have." He refuses even to imagine a utopia: "It's just a mere dream, 'everybody have the same thing,' just a foolish dream. I just hope for the future. That's the only way I could put it. You live on hope."

Conclusion: The Politics of Economic Redistribution

What can we learn about social justice from this excursion into the minds of two individuals with absolutely no political clout? If they are like other poor Americans, they lead us to a powerful conclusion about support for redistribution among the American poor. The poor do not oppose redistribution; they merely do not actively seek it. They hold beliefs about justice which inherently and fundamentally contradict each other. They need never confront the disjunction between economic differentiation and political equality so long as they keep the two domains separate in their minds and their daily lives. They accept and even support governmental influence in allocating quasi-material goods such as education and jobs. But when asked to consider political redistribution of income and wealth—explicitly material holdings coming directly from economic activity—they must face their normative disjunction between polity and economy. When they do so, they cannot philosophize their way out of it and are left with bitterness, despair, illogic, and denial. They do not oppose redistribution, but they cannot support it either.

This conclusion must be located in two contexts for its full implications to be clear. First, consider the location of individuals' beliefs in their social context. The poor do not develop their norms of justice, their contradictions, and their consequent inactivity, in a vacuum. The entire structure of American political thought and action revolves around keeping the economy separate from the polity. I have no room here to develop this assertion; suffice it to say that American liberal capitalism is dedicated to the propositions that economic activity should be insulated from political activity, and that economic justice is fundamentally different from political justice. These propositions can be evaluated two ways—as efforts to guarantee both political rights and equality *and* economic freedom,[13] or as a strategy to keep the poor not only poor but also convinced that they *should* be poor even though others are rich.[14] But so long as the American polity continues to ignore the intimate relation between economic well-being and political power, and continues to maintain contradictory beliefs about justice in the two domains, the American poor will continue to "oppose"—i.e., not to seek actively—the redistribution of wealth.

Second and finally, consider the location of American beliefs in an international context. This is the old and venerable question of American exceptionalism, here specified as: "Is the disjunction between economic and political norms, and its consequent muddle about redistribution, a peculiarly American phenomenon?" If, for example, European socialists hold a three-part pattern of beliefs similar to that of (non-socialist) Americans, then my findings do not explain the absence of socialism in the United States. Unfortunately we lack the data to determine whether this pattern is uniquely, not only profoundly, American. Furthermore, this too is an issue that can only be raised, not resolved, in an article of this length. Nevertheless, I can venture a few assertions of a comparative nature. English adolescents are less likely than American adolescents to perceive a class structure in their society and to locate themselves within it, but they are also less likely to attribute wealth to individual effort and poverty to laziness.[15] Americans "are somewhat more likely than the English to believe that they have or will 'really get ahead by earning a lot of money,' and in the United States such a belief is negatively correlated with...[support for] equality. Not so in England."[16] Americans are, however, more egalitarian than the British on some *political* questions.[17] Jamaican leaders are more egalitarian on some economic issues than American students, but more differentiating on others.[18] Americans identify more with their fellow citizens and less with members of their own class than residents of eight other advanced industrial nations.[19] The evidence overall is inconsistent and nonsystematic, but we can conclude at least that it is plausible that Americans are less egalitarian economically and more egalitarian politically than citizens of other nations.

We end, of course, with more questions than answers. Where do my respondents get their beliefs; how do American beliefs compare with other nations'; what is the connection between micro-level norms and macro-level political movements? But the question of "Why no socialism?" has advanced. Poor Americans oppose, in the special sense of not supporting, the redistribution of wealth because they cannot reconcile their irreconcilable beliefs in economic inequality and personal and political equality. Philosophical distinctions in norms of distributive justice translate, for them, into poverty, confusion, and political paralysis.

Politics Department
Princeton University

NOTES

1. Werner Sombart, *Why is There No Socialism in the United States?* trans. Patricia M. Hocking and C. T. Husbands (White Plains, New York: M. E. Sharpe, 1976).

2. In 1977, the median money income of households in the United States was $13,572; the mean income was $16,000. The difference was $2,528. In 1970, there was only a $1,978 gap (in 1977 dollars) between median and mean income. U.S. Bureau of the Census, "Money Income in 1977 of Households in the United States," *Current Population Reports*, P-60, no. 117 (Washington, D.C.: U.S. Government Printing Office, 1978), p. 2. This measure suggests what more sophisticated data confirm: income has become more unequally distributed since 1970.

3. U.S. Bureau of the Census, *Income Distribution in the United States*, by Herman P. Miller (Washington D.C.: U.S. Government Printing Office, 1966), p. 21; and U.S. Bureau of the Census, "Money Income in 1977," p. 19. Note that the Census Bureau assumes that households with incomes over $100,000 earn exactly $100,000. This assumption makes the shares of the wealthiest 20% and 5% in the text smaller than they actually are, since it measures the income of someone who actually makes $500,000 as only $100,000.

4. Adapted from Stanley Lebergott, *The American Economy* (Princeton, N.J.: Princeton University Press, 1976), p. 242.

5. Malcolm Sawyer, "Income Distribution in OECD Countries," *OECD Economic Outlook: Occasional Studies* (Paris: Organisation for Economic Co-operation and Development, 1976), p. 14.

6. "The Fortune Survey: XXII, *Fortune Magazine* (June 1939): 68.

7. Joseph Feagin, "Poverty: We Still Believe That God Helps Those Who Help Themselves," *Psychology Today* (November 1972) pp. 101ff.

8. Philip E. Converse, Jean D. Dotson, Wendy J. Hoag, and William H. McGee III, *American Social Attitudes Data Sourcebook, 1947-1978* (Cambridge, Mass.: Harvard University Press, 1980), pp. 385, 393, 397, 398.

9. Converse, *et al.*, pp. 377, 381, 409.

10. Warren E. Miller, Arthur H. Miller, and Edward J. Schneider, *American National Election Studies Data Sourcebook, 1952-1978* (Cambridge, Mass.: Harvard University Press,

1980), pp. 185, 189; Natalie Jaffe, "Attitudes Towards Public Welfare Programs and Recipients in the United States," Appendix B in Lester Salamon, *Welfare: the Elusive Consensus*
(New York: Praeger, 1978), pp. 221-28; Hazel Erskine, "The Polls: Health Insurance," *Public
Opinion Quarterly*, 39, no. 1 (Spring 1975): 128-43; and Hazel Erskine, "The Polls: Government Role in Welfare," *Public Opinion Quarterly*, 39, no. 2 (Summer 1975): 257-74.

11. Note that this paragraph discusses "people," not "the poor." I argue in my full work on
this subject that the American rich hold basically the same views on distributive justice as the
poor do, although their psychological and political responses to these beliefs differ considerably. Thus the explanatory variable of support for or opposition to equality in any particular choice is neither individual ideology nor class position, but rather the domain in which
that choice occurs. See Jennifer L. Hochschild, *What's Fair?: American Beliefs about
Distributive Justice* (Cambridge, Mass.: Harvard University Press, 1981).

12. One caveat here—using an egalitarian norm does not automatically imply that one seeks
to redistribute downward, and, correspondingly, using a differentiating norm does not
automatically imply that one seeks to redistribute upward. The distributive consequences of using a particular norm vary with the circumstances of its use.

13. For example, see Milton Friedman, *Capitalism and Freedom* (Chicago: University of
Chicago Press, 1962), pp. 1-36, and John Rawls, *A Theory of Justice* (Cambridge: Harvard
University Press, 1971), pp. 359-60.

14. For example, see Perry Anderson, "The Antinomies of Antonio Gramsci," *New Left
Review* 100 (November 1976-January 1977): 5-78. For a general, not specifically American,
version of this interpretation, see Frank Parkin, *Class Inequality and Political Order* (New
York: Praeger, 1971), esp. pp. 81-86.

15. Alan Stern and Donald Searing, "The Stratification Beliefs of English and American
Adolescents," *British Journal of Political Science* 6 (April 1976): 177-201. For claims that
Americans are less class-conscious than Britons, see Robert Robinson and Jonathon Kelley,
"Marx and Dahrendorf on Income Inequality, Class Consciousness, and Class Conflict: an
Empirical Test," paper presented at the annual meeting of the American Sociological Associa-
tion, Chicago, 1977.

16. Robert Robinson and Wendell Bell, "Equality, Success, and Social Justice in England
and the United States," *American Sociological Review* 43 (April 1978): 125-43. See also Ralph
Turner, "Acceptance of Irregular Mobility in Britain and the United States," *Sociometry* 29,
no. 4 (December 1966): 334-52.

17. Wendell Bell and Robert Robinson, "An Index of Evaluated Equality: Measuring Conceptions of Social Justice in England and the United States," in *Comparative Studies in
Sociology*, ed. Richard Tomasson (Greenwich, CT: JAI Press, 1978): I, 235-70.

18. Wendell Bell, *Jamaican Leaders* (Berkeley: University of California Press, 1964),
chapter 4.

19. Donald Devine, *The Political Culture of the United States* (Boston: Little, Brown,
1972), p. 95.

A NON-EGALITARIAN DEFENSE OF REDISTRIBUTION*

Christopher W. Morris

Many defenses of downward redistribution start from egalitarian premises; they assume a reduction of inequality and the attainment of greater equality to be goals intrinsically worthy of pursuit.[1] Many arguments against redistribution equate it with theft and the wrongful coercion of individuals.[2] Both of these positions strike me as wrong. Not all redistribution is theft—although redistribution for egalitarian reasons alone may very well be. I wish to defend some forms of downward redistribution and thus to demonstrate that it need not be theft, and I wish to do this without making any of the standard egalitarian assumptions. If my arguments are successful, then there is a liberal individualist defense of redistribution.

Redistribution is one of the major social issues of our time. It seems to be the main issue that divides contemporary conservatives, libertarians, and the liberal left.[3] To some, redistribution is what is wrong with the Welfare State. To others, the Welfare State does not redistribute enough.[4] But what exactly is at issue in these debates?

Let us define the notion. *Redistribution*, I shall say, *is a coercively imposed transfer of goods (or their equivalent in utility) from one person to another.*[5] The mention of coercion is crucial here. Since voluntary or noncoercive transfers occur all the time in ordinary human interaction, all exchange would be redistributive were we not to include the condition of coercion in our characterization of the notion. Surely voluntary alteration of the distribution of goods is not what is at issue here.

If I steal my neighbor's blender, and the judge orders me to return it, is this redistribution (or re-redistribution)? Let us call this *rectificatory redistribution*. Given criteria for just ownership, redistribution for reasons of rectification may be justified. Few social theorists will or could (in all honesty) object to such forms of redistribution.[6] Thus I do not think that it is issues concerning the restoration of stolen or unjustly acquired goods that divides political camps today, even though there is of course great dispute here. Rather, it would seem that it is non-rectificatory redistribution that is at issue (hereafter 'non-rectificatory' will be understood).

What about some of the programs of our welfare states, such as unemployment benefits or state-run health care programs? These typically redistribute (coercively). Are they what is at issue? Not necessarily.[7] Think of such programs as forms of collective charity or collective insurance. In recent decades many such programs have been defended by appeal to an acknowledged function of government, namely the collective provision of public goods.[8]

Distinguish between *cooperative* and *non-cooperative* redistribution. The latter is essentially zero- or negative-sum redistribution: some gain and some lose, and the losses balance out or exceed the gains. Cooperative redistribution, by contrast, benefits all involved; it is Pareto-efficient.[9] Suppose that all members of a large community wish to assist the poor of a neighboring community, who either are the victims of some unexpected catastrophe or simply are in an unfortunate situation. But no one in the wealthy community wishes to assist the poor unless everyone (or almost everyone) does, and further each has some reason to believe that others will seek to be "free riders" if there is no coordination of giving. Thus the local community government taxes the members of the wealthy group and distributes the fund to the poor. Redistribution here is essentially a public good in the technical sense: consumption is non-rival and users may not be excluded. Such are "Pareto-optimal redistributions."[10] Essentially this is cooperative redistribution: all members of the philanthropic wealthy community — as well as the recipients of the aid — benefit from the redistributive activity of their government.

Note an important feature of cooperative redistribution. The members of the wealthy community are obligated to one another to contribute to the redistribution fund, and each has a claim-right against the others that they also contribute. But the poor here are mere third-party beneficiaries. That is, they do not have a claim-right to the redistributed wealth, a claim-right that would obligate the members of the wealthy community to come to their aid. The poor here are beneficiaries of a collective charity administered by the government. As such they cannot claim a right[11] to the wealth in question (until, of course, the title to that wealth has been transferred to them).

This point is important for matters of justice. If one seeks to justify redistribution using such "cooperative" arguments, one will not be able to say that the potential recipients of the redistributed wealth have a claim-right to that wealth (prior to receiving it), a right which obligates each of the donors to give. All such redistributions will essentially be collective charity (or collective insurance; see below). Someone who seeks, as I do, to argue that potential recipients of (some forms of) redistribution have a claim-right to that redistribution must use other justifications.

Unemployment benefits, welfare for the very poor and for the disabled, and assistance to the victims of catastrophes may also be rationalized as a sort of compulsory insurance program.[12] We may each of us be victims of some catastrophe or accident and thus benefit from such "insurance," especially if we are risk-averse. Further, we may wish to collectivize the costs of such programs in ways not possible with private schemes, espcially since the latter always have the right to exclude some individuals.

The important feature of these forms of cooperative redistribution is that they involve public goods. In each, redistribution is a public good; all involved benefit, and they do so independently of their contribution to the costs of the program. Thus there is a widely accepted justification for invoking the coercive powers of the state in order to collectivize such programs (provided that *all* do benefit). Non-cooperative redistribution may not, however, be so easily justified. And it is clearly such redistribution that is at issue in contemporary political debate.

It is, then, non-cooperative (and non-rectificatory) redistribution that concerns us (hereafter I shall speak simply of redistribution). Before stating my two arguments for such redistribution, there are still further preliminary clarifications to be made. *Re*distribution is always redistributive relative to some specific distribution of goods, relative to some (temporally or conceptually) prior state of affairs.

Let us define a *status-quo-superseding redistribution*, as a coercively imposed alteration of the existing distribution of goods (or their equivalent in utility), where such an alteration is non-rectificatory and non-cooperative. I shall be arguing that some such downward status quo redistributions are justified. However, even this notion of redistribution, or rather this baseline for determining redistributions, does not bring out what upsets many social critics. Critics could not (consistently) condemn redistribution and then go on to recommend abolition of welfare state "redistribution" if they set up the status quo as the relevant baseline. For then it would be they, and not the defenders of the welfare state, who would be proponents of redistribution. It would seem that the relevant baseline distribution for many discussions is that (counter-factual) distribution of goods (or utility) that would come about in a free market, one without many of the features of contemporary mixed economies.

Economists of the neo-classical persuasion frequently use models that suppose that individuals are rational in the sense of maximizing subjective utility, that they are free to produce and exchange as they wish (subject to constraints against force and fraud), and that all factors and products are privately owned. Further, they suppose that all utility functions are independent and that there are no public goods or externalities (uncompensated benefits or costs). Such are called "perfectly competitive markets." Now some economists seem to discuss (and condemn) redistribution relative to the distribution of goods attained by agents interacting in accordance with the constraints of such perfectly competitive markets. Welfare payments to the poor, or to the rich or middle-classes (as is so often the case), are thus redistributive since they are coercively imposed transfers relative to a perfectly competitive market baseline. Although many economists of this persuasion condemn such redistribution as inefficient, in the Pareto sense, others will openly object on moral grounds as well.[13] Let us call this type of redistribution, *market-superseding,* defining it thus: a coercively imposed transfer of goods (or utility) of agents who have interacted in accordance with the constraints of a perfectly competitive market. (Adding that such redistribution is non-cooperative or non-rectificatory would be redundant since in such markets, by hypothesis, there is no call for collective provision of public goods or for rectification of wrongs.)

One further remark. While it seems that many social critics implicitly employ the perfect market baseline for judgments about redistribution, mention of initial assets above should alert the reader to the fact that this baseline is incomplete and thus cannot, without further specification, carry all the normative weight that these critics wish to accord it. For the counterfactual 'distribution of goods in a perfectly competitive market' is empirically empty until the distribution of initial assets is specified. After all, different distributions of goods will obtain depending on the initial distribution of assets.[14] If normative weight is to be accorded this baseline, then critics cannot dodge the matter of specifying initial assets and hence of entering into a moral discussion about the justice of different initial distributions.

To summarize this rather lengthy introduction, what seems to be at issue in contemporary debates about redistribution is non-rectificatory, non-cooperative redistribution. Such redistributions seem usually to be thought of as alterations either of the status quo or of the distribution that would come about were individuals interacting subject only to the constraints of a perfectly competitive market. Since we live in market societies, although not perfectly competitive ones, both baselines raise important questions about the justice of market distributions of goods.

I shall now put forward an argument for downward redistribution. If successful, this argument will justify both market-superseding and status-quo-superseding redistribution, although the practical import of the latter depends on a specification of what constitutes the status quo distribution, a task I shall not attempt here. Further, if successful, this argument will justify attributing a claim-right to the potential recipients of such redistribution; the redistribution justified will not be of the collective charity variety. Lastly, if successful, this argument will constitute a non-egalitarian justification of redistribution since no appeal will be made to assumptions foreign to the liberal individual tradition common to most social theorists of the libertarian and liberal spectrum of the political continuum.[15]

The argument will be developed for a society in which a market exists, but a market that is "imperfectly competitive." I could furnish a similar argument assuming a perfectly competitive market, though perfect competition is a fiction of textbooks. In that argument,[16] I would show that even if, in view of the fact that any distribution of goods brought about by such a market would be the result of the free and informed choices of rational individuals, given their preferences, assets, and endowments, a perfectly competitive market is accepted as "justice-preserving,"[17] just if the preceding distribution was just, it does not follow that the present result is just. For the history of the market may not be such as to be consistent with the supposition that it arose from a just pre-market distribution. Every successive distribution in the history of a perfectly competitive market may have been unjust because the market began with an unjust distribution.

So, of course, might an "imperfectly competitive" market. What would a just pre-market distribution be? Let us assume a general contractarian principle of justice, namely, that a state of affairs is just if and only if it is mutually advantageous to all members and thus could have been the outcome of a hypothetical agreement in a state of nature between those agents.[18] Then I argue that a just pre-market distribution would be more egalitarian than the present distribution of goods, as well as more egalitarian than any pre-market distribution that can plausibly be postulated as an historical origin for the present market.

Assume that Alvin and Beatrice are in a state of nature—that is, a state temporally or conceptually prior to markets and governments—and that they are not equal in the amount of effort they must each expend to produce the goods they want. Acting independently, each produces a certain quantity of goods depending on effort. This is illustrated by Figure 1, with effort measured along the vertical axis, goods along the horizontal axis.[19] Alvin's production function, if he acts independently of Beatrice, is shown by curve P_a, Beatrice's production function in the same circumstances is shown by P_b. One might follow natural rights libertarians and identify the baseline for market interaction with the holdings that Alvin and Beatrice have as determined by their individual efforts in such a state of nature. Assume that

Alvin is satisfied with expending e units of effort for a return of 1 unit of goods, and that Beatrice is satisfied with f units of effort for 5 units of goods, each having different production functions. (Assuming that both have identical production functions makes the argument for redistribution very simple.) We could identify the just baseline for market interaction with the "Lockean" holdings that each has at $(e, 1)$ and $(f, 5)$ respectively. This is essentially the move that natural rights libertarians make, with a few complications aside.[20]

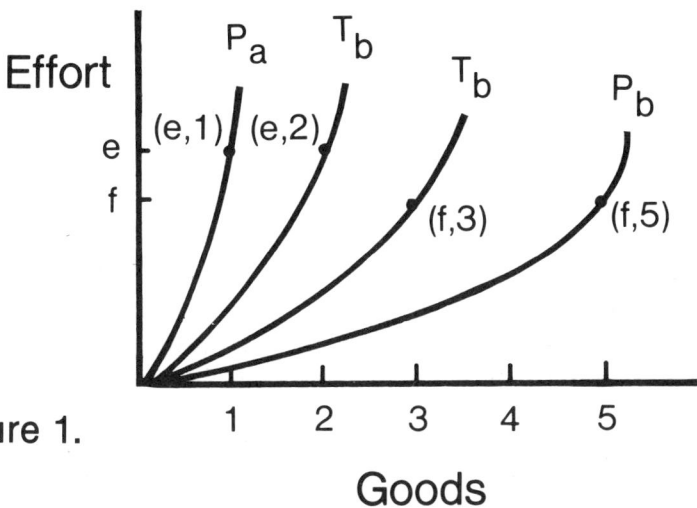

Figure 1.

Such a baseline may not be just, however, for it need not be mutually acceptable.[21] Assume that Alvin and Beatrice can change their holdings simply by taking some of the other's possessions. Their production functions, with predatory and defense efforts and gains included, may then be different. Let T_a and T_b represent these new functions. With the same amount of effort, let us say that Alvin can obtain 2 units of goods (instead of 1), while Beatrice obtains 3 (instead of 5). Why draw the new functions thus? Why not assume that Beatrice, the more effective producer, is also a more effective predator? My reason for drawing the functions in this manner is that the more effective producer has more possessions and assets to protect, all other things being equal, and thus is more vulnerable to predation. Beatrice, while better endowed with human capital—I do not assume equality of talents here—is wealthier, possesses more non-human capital, than Alvin; she is thus more vulnerable to predation than he. Further, it is security of possessions afforded by independent action, or, in civil society, by enforced property rights, that allows Beatrice to accumulate as much as she does in the world represented by P_a and P_b. Without security for independent action the inability to be secure in the fruits of her superior productive capacities and consequently the inability to plan much for the future severely limit Beatrice's productivity. Even without assuming equality of talents (as Hobbes does), it seems clear that the net social product of individuals in a state of nature with predatory and defensive interaction will be much smaller than that of a (Lockean) state with non-interacting individuals.[22]

Let us then represent Alvin and Beatrice's production functions in a state with predatory and defensive interaction as T_a and T_b respectively. Assuming that each chooses to maintain the same amount of effort — simplifying by assuming few incentive effects — why should we assume that the just initial state for market interaction legitimate the "Lockean" holdings of each — $(e, 1)$ and $(f, 5)$ — rather than the "Hobbesian" holdings that each obtains when predatory and defense efforts are taken into account — $(e, 2)$ and $(f, 3)$?

If we do not presuppose any moral constraints prior to agreement in this state — that is, if we identify the initial baseline for market interaction with the baseline of moral interaction[23] — then the distribution represented by $(e, 2)$ and $(f, 3)$ should be the favored candidate for a just initial state. Recalling that a competitive market requires the absence of force and fraud, the fulfillment of contracts, and the respect of private property, it should be clear that determining the legitimate initial holdings of individuals by reference to what they acquire independently of one another — as determined by functions P_a and P_b — would not be acceptable to Alvin in our example. He would not accept to abide by the constraints of a perfectly competitive market if the initial distribution were determined by P_a and P_b, since he can do better. For him, the "Hobbesian" holdings as determined by T_a and T_b are the relevant initial state, and given the absence of moral constraints on state of nature interactions, Alvin can shift the initial distribution to that one which he favors the most.[24] Why is this? Why does the "least advantaged" have the power to select the baseline? Either party has the power to shift the baseline from $(e, 1)$ $(f, 5)$ to $(e, 2)$, $(f, 3)$, since such a shift may be made *unilaterally*. However, only the least advantaged, namely Alvin, has an incentive to do so. The predatory baseline, unlike the "Lockean" baseline, is not maintained by cooperation; it is thus more stable.

The initial, pre-market baseline that is likely to emerge as the stable and mutually advantageous starting point will be more egalitarian than the

"Lockean" alternative. The most advantaged would clearly prefer the "Lockean" baseline, but in the absence of binding moral constraints, she can give no good reason to the least advantaged to prevent him from shifting back toward the "Hobbesian" predatory baseline. (Perhaps Beatrice and Alvin can negotiate a baseline mid-point between the two I specified; but it should be clear that Alvin's power to shift to the "Hobbesian" point determines the baseline for this negotiation.) If we take seriously the likely efficiency costs created by the predatory and defense activities of our two characters, the mutually agreeable initial state is likely to be even more egalitarian yet since the net joint product will be very small (smaller than the 5 units of goods that are created in the predatory state our friends find themselves in). Thus, even if we do not assume that individuals are very similar in natural endowment (as Hobbes assumes), the just initial or pre-trade distribution is likely to be highly egalitarian because of the least advantaged's power to determine the baseline (but also because of the small size of the net joint product).

Effects persisting from an unjust pre-market distribution supply one target for redistribution in an egalitarian direction. While it is clear that a perfectly competitive market with an equal distribution of pre-trade assets will generate unequal holdings after trade if we assume that individual preferences differ (as well as different productive capacities), the fact of an equal (or roughly equal) pre-trade distribution creates a rationale for redistribution of the outcome of perfect competition (and the status quo distribution) if we grant that this just and relatively equal pre-trade distribution did not obtain in the initial, pre-trade states of real markets. The opportunity to internalize the significant externalities present in an imperfectly competitive market — if the opportunity is exploited, as it should be, in a way properly founded on the idea just arrived at of what a just pre-market distribution would be — supplies a further opportunity for just redistribution, again in an egalitarian direction.

Real markets do not fulfill many of the conditions necessary for a perfectly competitive optimum. Significant externalities, for instance, exist and these prevent the market equilibrium from being Pareto-efficient. Air and water pollution are standard examples, but force and fraud, sometimes employed by individuals who cloak themselves in talk about the virtues of free markets, are also significant externalities in our societies. The existence of important public goods, such as national defense (a public bad for some?), a safe environment, or preservation of natural resources, make existing markets less than "perfect." The resolution of serious externalities and the provision (though not necessarily the production) of public goods are usually acknowledged by critics of redistribution to be important and legitimate functions of government.[25] In an imperfectly competitive market a new distribution of goods (via the creation and distribution of new property rights in previously unowned things) will internalize significant externalities and thereby make everyone affected better off.

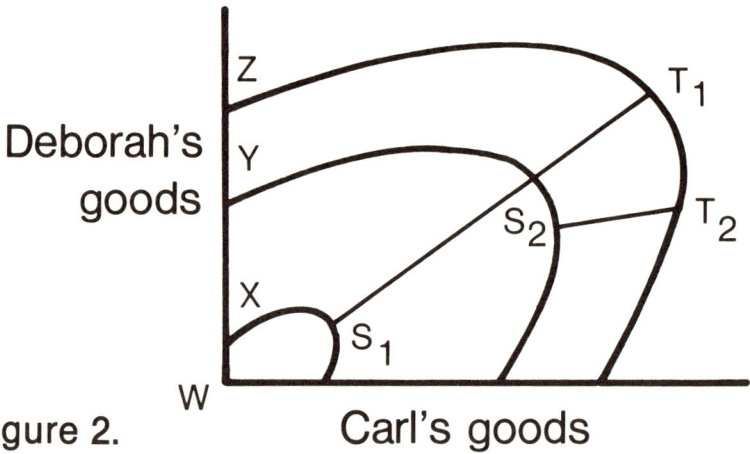

Figure 2.

Suppose that Carl and Deborah are interacting in an imperfectly competitive market represented by Figure 2. The possible distributions of goods are represented by curves showing the different quantities of goods available to Carl and Deborah respectively. Let curve Z represent the possible distributions available to Carl and Deborah should they reach an agreement to internalize significant externalities. Carl and Deborah find themselves in an imperfectly competitive market, at point S_2 on the graph; S_2 is the market equilibrium point lying on a curve Y of possible distributions available to our two friends. Carl and Deborah seek to internalize existing externalities. Accordingly, they wish to reach an agreement about the distribution of goods that will do this best. What is the baseline from which such an agreement should be made? There are at least three relevant ones. First, there is S_2, the market equilibrium at which Carl and Deborah find themselves. Secondly, there is that baseline which I shall call "Hobbesian anarchy" (the counterpart to the predatory baseline in my first argument), which is represented below by S_1 on curve X; curve X represents the possible distributions of goods in the two person state of nature where Carl and Deborah act unconstrained by moral (or market) rules, and S_1 represents the "natural equilibrium"[26] reached in that state. And thirdly, there is the point W which is that state where Carl and Deborah have no goods at all.

We need not pause with W as a candidate for the relevant baseline. Readers may recognize that this is essentially the baseline for contractual agreement that Rawls uses in his theory.[27] Which of the other baselines, S_1 or S_2, is the relevant one for negotiations for internalizing significant externalities? Let us suppose that T_1 is a point on the distribution curve Z and represents the distribution of goods that Carl and Deborah would agree on were they to negotiate using S_1 as their baseline, and that T_2 is that distribution reached by agreement from S_2. Now it may not make any difference which of the two baselines Carl and Deborah select. Suppose that our two friends are in a contractarian original position — with general knowledge about societies, similar to that possessed by Rawlsian contractors — at S_1 and that they select the fundamental norms and rules that will everafter constrain their behavior. Granting them perfect information, they know that any society in which they live will have externalities which they will want to be able to resolve. So at S_1 they agree upon rules and institutions that will allow them to internalize future externalities later on, say at S_2. Thus T_1 will be reached whether Carl and Deborah are negotiating from S_1 or S_2. It will not matter which we select as the relevant baseline. The reason for this is that our protagonists, in their foresight (built into the model by the condition of perfect information), have devised and agreed to rules and institutions that enable them, at a later date, to internalize externalities at S_2 and to reach T_1.

Suppose, however, that S_2 does not include those ideal collective choice mechanisms, that Carl and Deborah do not possess perfect knowledge about human history and societies (either here or in an original position), and hence that they did not have the foresight to agree to rules for internalizing all externalities they would encounter later. I take it that this is something like the situation we are in, where not only markets "imperfect" but collective choice mechanisms and political institutions are so as well. Most of our political institutions were developed years ago and do not work especially well given changes that probably could not have been anticipated earlier. Further, these institutions themselves generate unanticipated externalities. Forgetting then about perfect knowledge and "perfect" institutions suppose instead that Carl and Deborah find themselves at S_2 along with a set of "imperfect" political institutions. And suppose that were they to bargain within the constraints of S_2 and of its rules they would reach T_2 (instead of T_1 which they would reach bargaining from S_1). Now the problem of the baseline arises. Given the manner in which I have set up the example, it will be in Deborah's interest to shift the baseline back toward S_1, whereas

Carl has an interest in bargaining from S_2 (and in having Deborah respect the constraints of S_2). S_2 as a baseline favors Carl, S_1 favors Deborah.

I would suggest that the solution in this case involves a shift back toward S_1. Once again, the "worst-off" member of our little society has a bargaining advantage in the selection of baselines.[28] Again the wealthier Carl, having more assets to protect, is more vulnerable than Deborah; the more the former's assets depend on the stability of the social and legal framework (e.g., stocks and bonds), the more vulnerable his wealth will be to threatened returns to Hobbesian anarchy. And Deborah can unilaterally shift the baseline back to S_1.[29] S_2 contains certain constraints, especially laws involving private property, which it is no longer advantageous for Deborah to adhere to as long as the matter of moving to curve Z is being decided. Now any distribution approximating T_1 will appear redistributive if one takes S_2 as the relevant baseline; indeed any such distribution will be both status quo and market redistributive of S_2. Those who take S_2 as the relevant baseline for negotiations, the defenders of the status quo, must view the move toward T_1 as redistributive. If we complicate the example with the addition of explicitly different utility and production functions for Carl and Deborah, and take into account the efficiency effects of both the redistribution and the absence of redistribution,[30] results may be even more redistributive.

Thus, the internalization of important, unanticipated externalities provides an occasion and justification for measures redistributive both of the status quo and of market distributions of goods. Further, such redistributions favor the "worst-off" in society—the position held by Deborah in our example—since they possess the bargaining advantage in determining the baseline for negotiation. Why should the worst-off comply with the basic rules governing, say, property rights given their enormous disruptive power in any complex society. After all, the well-off favor the status quo (S_2) as the relevant baseline for internalizing externalities since their bargaining advantage here (at S_2) enables them to reach an advantageous settlement (T_2). But they do not have the last word in determining the baseline, as we have seen. Another way of viewing this form of redistribution is simply as a way of ensuring that the fundamental rules and institutions are mutually advantageous to all, mutual advantage being determined from the Hobbesian baseline (S_1).[31] Each individual should have (or be given) reasons, in terms of his or her interests, to prefer complying with the rules and institutions of society than shifting back to a state of nature.

I conclude, then, my argument. What implications does this argument have for our world? This is the important question, after all; unfortunately it is the most difficult question, and I cannot hope to say anything very complete here. I would think that the argument might justify much of the redistribution to the poor that is characteristic, say, of the U.S. and Canada today. This is not to endorse the possibly greater redistribution that benefits the middle classes, tobacco and peanut farmers, truckers, houseowners, stockholders of Chrysler, etc. Nor is it to defend the particular form taken by redistributive programs that are intended for the very poor. Economists and others frequently draw attention to the inefficiencies of such programs (as well, of course, as that of those intended for the not-so-poor). Since many such economists seek to discredit all forms of redistribution (market or status quo redistribution?) by pointing out inefficiencies, social theorists (especially egalitarians)[32] tend to ignore all such problems and studies.

Efficiency problems are, however, very important. It seems clear that the size of the social pie, to use that notorious redistributive metaphor,[33] *is* severely shrunk by large redistributions. While it is also true that the perception on the part of individuals that their social order is a fair one, and consequently the redistribution necessary to realize this are important to general efficiency, there are undoubtedly limits to how much actual redistribution can be carried out without adversely affecting incentives even if agreement to redistribute is widely shared.

Further, redistributive mechanisms create incentives to invest resources in "rent-seeking," that, is in obtaining goods through the redistributive mechanisms of the state.[34] It is already clear that many large interests other than the very poor are already very able at this game. One need merely notice the large corporate offices in Washington and Ottawa to gain an understanding of the investment now made in attempts to influence political decisions. The defenders of the poor are not beginners at this art either, but it is not clear that their clients are the main beneficiaries of their lobbying activities.

Lastly, while I have been discussing redistribution within a national context, it is worrisome to realize that when we think about the issues I have been discussing on an international scale, it is not at all clear what (if any) forms of redistribution should be effected.

All these facts are practical worries and not ethical arguments against redistribution, *contra* those social critics who use them as such. They are, however, serious practical problems with the implementation of the redistribution for which I have argued. We may wish to conjoin to our defense of redistribution a proviso to the effect that just redistribution should be carried out only up to the point where recipients start becoming worse-off than they otherwise would be. But that is a matter for another essay.

If my arguments are sound, a non-egalitarian, liberal individualist case can be made for (non-rectificatory, non-cooperative) redistribution. We need not embrace an egalitarianism to justify redistribution.

Department of Government
University of Texas at Austin

NOTES

* Hilliard Aronovitch, Andrew Lugg, and Adam Morton commented on a distant ancestor of this essay, and I am grateful for their help. The discussion at the Bowling Green Conference on Social Justice was also very useful and I thank the participants. David Gauthier, Wayne Sumner, and one of the two anonymous referees for *Ethics* have provided me with extensive written criticisms which I have sought to meet in this version of the essay. One criticism that my argument collapses with the introduction of coalitions (and of *n*-person models), I cannot meet without moving away from the "natural distribution" baseline that I borrow from James Buchanan. But I am coming to believe that there are independent reasons for extensively modifying this notion. I am also grateful to Michael Bradie and David Braybrooke for some suggested revisions.

1. See, for instance, Arthur M. Okun, *Equality or Efficiency: The Big Tradeoff* (Washington, D.C.: The Brookings Institution, 1975), pp. 1-31; Lester C. Thurow, *Generating Inequality: Mechanisms of Distribution in the U.S. Economy* (New York: Basic Books, 1975), pp. 20-50; Michael Walzer, "In Defense of Equality," in *Radical Principles* (New York: Basic Books, 1980), pp. 237-56; and Bernard Williams, "The Idea of Equality," in *Problems of the Self* (Cambridge; Cambridge University Press, 1973), pp. 230-49.

2. See, for instance, Milton Friedman, *Capitalism and Freedom* (Chicago: University of Chicago Press, 1962), p. 174; and Robert Nozick, *Anarchy, State, and Utopia* (New York: Basic Books,. 1974), pp. 167-74.

3. By conservative, I mean social theorists such as W. Buckley, I. Kristol, and R. Nisbet; by libertarian (or classical liberal), M. Friedman, R. Nozick, and M. Rothbard; and by the liberal left, R. Dworkin, A. M. Okun, J. Rawls, and L. Thurow. It seems to me very important not to follow the contemporary American practice of lumping the first two groups together. Of course, redistributive issues divide the socialist left from these other groups also.

4. To still others, the Welfare State redistributes to the wrong group, namely the middle classes. See George Stigler, "Director's Law of Public Income Redistribution," *Journal of Law and Economics* 13 (1970), 1-10; Gordon Tullock, "The Charity of the Uncharitable," *Western Economic Journal* IX (1971), 379-92 and "The Rhetoric and Reality of Redistribution," *Southern Economic Journal* 47 (1981), 895-907. See also Nozick, pp. 274-75. However, see the critical remarks of Gian Singh Sahota, "Theories of Personal Income Distribution: A Survey," *Journal of Economic Literature* XVI (1978), esp. pp. 29-30, and Edgar K. Browning,

Redistribution and the Welfare System (Washington, D.C.: American Enterprise Institute, 1975), esp. pp. 28-29. Browning elsewhere makes the point, confirmed by my investigations of the literature, that

> it is extremely difficult to take the broad view of the welfare system in this country. This difficulty is due to the fact that the system is so complex no one can understand it fully. The present system is composed of perhaps a dozen quantitatively important programs, and another 200 or so minor programs that interact and overlap in ways so bewildering that no one has ever been able to put together a coherent overview of the whole system. At least it is clear that nowhere in the literature is there a coherent picture of how all of these programs fit together and what their overall consequences are.
>
> For example, no one, to my knowledge, knows with any degree of accuracy how much income is redistributed annually to low-income families. One can find a number of very crude estimates... but these estimates are recognized as extraordinarily rough, and it is obvious that we do not really know exactly how much redistribution is going on in the present system.

Income Redistribution, Colin Campbell, ed. (Washington, D.C.: American Enterprise Institute, 1977), p. 208. See also Kenneth Boulding and Martin Pfaff, eds., *Redistribution to the Rich and the Poor* (Belmont, CA: Wadsworth Publishing, 1972); Sheldon Danziger, Robert Haveman, and Robert Plotnick, "How Income Transfers Affect Work, Savings, and the Income Distribution," *Journal of Economic Literature* XIX (1981), 975-1028; Sar Levitan, *Programs in Aid of the Poor for the 1980's* (Baltimore: Johns Hopkins University Press, 1980); and Paul Taubman, *Income Distribution and Redistribution* (Reading, MA and Menlo Park, CA: Addison-Wesley Publishing, 1978). Part of the difficulty of determining the amount of redistribution that takes place, say, in the U.S. today is that of including the value of in-kind transfers in one's estimates. Of course, much redistribution takes places through the use of tax breaks, protective barriers, and the public financing of public (*and* private) goods, and one despairs of ever being able to determine the precise amount of transfers that are effected in these (intentionally?) less obvious manners.

5. Usually legitimate redistributions, I shall assume, are to be carried out by the state or some legitimate political authority. But so as not to prejudge the case against Robin Hood, I do not include any such condition in the definition.

6. Even Nozick's theory allows for extensive rectification of past wrongs: "Although to introduce socialism as the punishment for our sins would be to go too far, past injustices might be so great as to make necessary in the short run a more extensive state in order to rectify them." Nozick, p. 231. Given the means our Western European ancestors used to appropriate North America, it may be that a great deal of rectificatory redistribution may be justified by Nozick's theory. On these issues see David Lyons, "The New Indian Claims and Original Rights to Land," *Social Theory and Practice* 4 (1977), 249-72; Michael McDonald, "Aboriginal Rights," in *Contemporary Issues in Political Philosophy*, W. R. Shea and J. King-Farlow, eds. (New York: Science History Publications, 1976), 432-35; and George Sher, "Ancient Wrongs and Modern Rights," *Philosophy and Public Affairs* 10 (1981), 3-17. See also my "Existential Limits to the Rectification of Past Wrongs" (unpublished) where I argue that such rectification is very limited due to the fact that most of the claimants would not have existed in the absence of the original wrong and thus have no claim to compensation.

7. See Marc F. Plattner, "The Welfare State vs. the Redistributive State," *The Public Interest* 55 (1979), 28-48. Actually I believe Plattner is mistaken in his distinction between the welfare and redistributive states.

8. A *public good* in the economic sense is a good whose availability to one person does not preclude its availability to others. The important characteristic of a public good is its indivisibility or non-rivalry. While the collective or state provision of public goods is acknowledged by most social theorists as legitimate—provided the social costs of state intervention are not greater than the social costs of foregoing the public good—most libertarians in the natural rights tradition dissent. Nozick, Rothbard, and others are clear in not allowing the state to provide public goods since such activity would violate the natural rights of individuals. Other libertarians, such as F. A. Hayek and M. Friedman, allow for the collective provision of such goods, but this merely reveals that they do not employ a natural rights normative theory. It will become clear that my general case for redistribution will not be effective against a natural rights opponent. But as my arguments will be implicitly contractarian, this is to be expected.

9. A state of affairs is Pareto-efficient (or Pareto-optimal) iff it is not possible to improve any one person's situation without making at least one other person worse off.

10. See H. M. Hochman and J. D. Rodgers, "Pareto Optimal Redistribution," *American Economic Review* 49 (1969), 542-56. See also the remarks by Friedman, pp. 191-92. See also L. Thurow. "The Income Distribution as a Pure Public Good," *Quarterly Journal of Economics* 85 (1971), 327-36.

11. I am speaking of a *right* in the sense of a claim entailing a correlative obligation on the part of some other to provide the charity. Such rights are to be carefully distinguished from Hohfeldian liberties (or privileges) which do not entail any such obligations on the part of others.

12. James Buchanan and Gordon Tullock, *The Calculus of Consent* (Ann Arbor, MI: University of Michigan Press, 1962), pp. 195-97; and Robert E. Goodin, *The Politics of Rational Man* (New York: John Wiley & Sons, 1976), esp. pp. 112, 115. See also Geoffrey Brennan, "Pareto Desirable Redistribution: The Non-Altruistic Dimension," *Public Choice* 14 (1973), pp. 43-67. While I may not be familiar with the relevant literature, it seems to me that this idea has not generated the interest that it deserves, especially compared to the interest sparked by that of Pareto-efficient redistribution. Further, the collective insurance rationale *may* entail a claim-right on the part of recipients to assistance.

13. See Friedman, p. 174.

14. If it is unlikely that even an equal initial distribution of assets will give rise, over time, to an equal distribution of goods—that is, equal distributions are unstable—then the incomplete baseline is not completely empty. One could use such a baseline to criticize strict egalitarians, for instance, without needing to specify the initial distribution.

15. Although my arguments are implicitly contractarian, and thus do not rest on utilitarian or natural rights assumptions, I view them as consistent with much of the liberal individualist tradition that starts with Hobbes and Adam Smith and runs all the way to Friedman, Hayek, and Rawls. Natural rights theorists, as I have already mentioned, will not be persuaded by my arguments, but then I am not persuaded that there are any natural rights.

16. Such an argument is developed in a longer version of this essay.

17. In effect such a market resolves the problem faced by non-moral agents in a Hobbesian state of nature, namely, their interactions do not lead to a Pareto-efficient equilibrium. I am indebted to David Gauthier for the idea that perfectly competitive markets are justice-preserving. The notion of "justice-preservation" itself comes from Nozick.

18. Readers familiar with the contemporary contractarian literature will recognize immediately the inadequacies of this general principle. Nonetheless, without being sidetracked into a discussion of contractarian justice, it is worthwhile stating a general principle, albeit in an inadequate way, for the purposes of my general argument.

19. I borrow here and elsewhere from Buchanan, *Limits of Liberty*.

20. One of these complications is the "Lockean Proviso." See Nozick, pp. 174-82.

21. See note 18.

22. This may not hold with coalitions.

23. A Hobbesian or contractarian assumption.

24. Even if we do not identify the baseline of market interaction with that of moral interaction, the "Lockean" holdings favored by natural rights theorist will not emerge as the relevant just baseline for market interaction; in this situation a compromise between the "Hobbesian" and "Lockean" baselines will most naturally be selected. (I shall not attempt to show this here.)

25. Friedman, of course, grants this. See Friedman, pp. 22-36. He is only following Adam Smith here; see the *Wealth of Nations* (New York: Modern Library, 1965 [1776]), p. 651. Natural rights theorists again will dissent.

It is interesting to note that the resolution of serious externalities in an imperfectly competitive market is structurally identical to the resolution of the problem facing rational individuals in a Hobbesian, non-moral state of nature. In the latter, the counterparts to air and water pollution are the externalities of force and fraud. Mutually advantageous arrangements giving rise to enforceable rights will "internalize" both sorts of externalities. I develop this point in "Moral Constraints, Prisoners' Dilemmas, and the Social Responsibilities of Corporations" (forthcoming).

26. See Buchanan, *Limits of Liberty*, ch. 4.

27. Critics have noted that use of this point as a baseline for negotiations presupposes that the initial agreement concerns the distribution of the net social product, rather than the *surplus* that remains when one subtracts from this net product the sum of the returns of individuals acting independently in the state of nature. W as a baseline assumes that the returns from no agreement are zero, which need not be the case. See Gauthier, "Justice and Natural Endowment," *Social Theory and Practice* 3 (1974), and Nozick, p. 184. But see also Buchanan, "A Hobbesian Interpretation of the Rawlsian Difference Principle," in his *Freedom and Constitutional Contract* (College Station, TX: Texas A & M University Press, 1977), pp. 194-211.

28. See the essay by Buchanan mentioned in note 27.

29. What if T_1 is to the right of T_2, i.e., less egalitarian? Then Deborah will have no incentive to shift the baseline back to S_1. Further, as I have drawn curve Z, any T to the right of T_2 will be Pareto-dominated by T_2. Assume that this is not the case, that curve Z extends to the southeast of T_2. Then *Carl* will shift back to S_1 if T_1 is to the southeast of T_2! But such a possibility strikes me as implausible given the greater dependence of the wealthy on the maintenance of established property rules and social order.

30. It is clear that redistributive programs have significant efficiency effects, and that it is important for defenders not to ignore these. However, the foregoing of just redistribution and the conviction on the part of individuals that the social order as a whole does not represent a fair bargain may also have important efficiency effects.

31. This view of redistribution is implicit, I believe, in the idea of a society as "a cooperative venture for mutual advantage." See Rawls, *A Theory of Justice* (Cambridge, MA: Harvard University Press, 1971), p. 4.

32. Exceptions are Okun, Rawls, and Thurow.

33. See Nozick, pp. 149-50.

34. See James Buchanan, Robert Tollison, and Gordon Tullock, eds., *Toward a Theory of the Rent-Seeking Society* (College Station, TX: Texas A & M University Press, 1980).

SOCIAL JUSTICE: WHAT IT IS AND WHY IT MATTERS

Hugo Adam Bedau

> "...the prevailing belief in 'social justice' is at present probably the gravest threat to most other values of a free civilization.... [T]he phrase 'social justice'...has become a dishonest insinuation that one ought to agree to a demand of some special interest which can give no reason for it."
>
> —F. A. von Hayek, *The Mirage of Social Justice* (1976), pp. 66-67, 97.

I

In a conference such as this, expressly devoted to the topic and the problems of social justice, it cannot be wholly inappropriate or trivial to devote some attention to whether there *is* any such topic or problems in the first place. The sentiments expressed in the epigraph above are obviously not universally shared, but they arise out of legitimate concerns and express, however offensively, considerations that we ignore at our peril. I shall resist the temptation to devote my efforts here to a polemical rebuttal of such hostile and misconceived attacks as that of von Hayek's. The most effective way to deal with the claims that there is no such thing as social justice, or at least nothing apart from what "envy and sentimentality can concoct,"[1] is to try to state directly the nature and the importance of social justice, and thus of theories of social justice.

Yet to try to do this immediately presents a problem, because the self-designated theorists of social justice are by no means in agreement as to what their theories are about. *Social* justice seems obviously in implicit contrast with *individual* justice, and sometimes this contrast is made explicit;[2] perhaps it is also to be contrasted with *legal* or formal justice.[3] Beyond this the going quickly becomes difficult. How in particular is social justice supposed to be related to classic *distributive* justice? For some philosophers, there is but one topic, which can be referred to indifferently as "distributive" or as "social" justice.[4] Rawls, for example, is one of those who goes to some pains to contrast the two and prefers to refer to his own theory as a theory of "social justice,"[5] something his critics regularly fail even to notice.[6] Perhaps it doesn't really matter. In any case, it is tempting to exit with the observation that the phrase, "social justice," as it is actually used today, is nothing more than a chapter-heading term denoting a congeries of doctrines, topics, and projects with no guiding thread among them and no organizing scheme holding them together.

Is there any way to improve on this vagueness and arbitrariness so that contemporary discussions of social justice can be brought into focus? In what follows I shall try. I propose to explain what social justice is and why it is important by reference to the way it brings into prominence *human needs* as such and as part of the proper subject-matter of justice. By human needs as such I do not refer to what are now called "special needs," a topic of much concern in the theory of just health care delivery. I mean rather the needs that any normal human being can be said to have. These needs are, of course, not easily specified with any precision independently of the social conditions in which they arise. Furthermore, they can be satisfied independently of social, political, and economic institutions hardly at all. It is inevitable, therefore, that a concern for the proper satisfaction of human needs will become a theory of a just society, of just social institutions, and thus a theory of *social* justice. There, in a nutshell, is the conception I shall try to elucidate in what follows.

II

Traditionally, basic human needs were directly taken into account in moral theory solely by reference to what Kant called "duties of imperfect obligation." As Kant might have put it, all persons have a duty (Christians would have called it the duty of charity) to perform acts of altruistic beneficence. The objects of such charity would be, strictly, the unmet needs of others. But to Kant, at least, it was perfectly clear that this duty was not a duty of justice. Instead, it was an "imperfect duty," in that the occasions of its performance were determined by inclination and choice of the agent, and not by right of the recipient.[7] Thus, human needs no matter how basic were never a basis in themselves for the needy person to have a claim of justice against some other person, or against any of the many, who could meet those needs. No one could be said to *owe* to another what would suffice for the latter's needs, and no one in need could on that ground *demand* or *claim as of right* what he needed from another. Consequently, one person's needs as such were the source of no more than a weak moral claim upon another person. Desert, merit, rights—only these could be the source of the stringent moral claims regulated by the principles of justice. This view, as we shall see shortly, has by no means died out. On the contrary, many social philosophers still adhere to it as a fixed principle of any possible theory of justice.

Against this background, it is easy to see one merit in utilitarianism, a merit, moreover, too readily overlooked by its many critics (among whom I count myself). For the utilitarian in moral theory, the discontent and misery from unmet needs is on exactly the same footing as the discontent and misery arising from unrequited desert, uncompensated rights-violations, disappointed expectations, as well as from other causes unrelated to putative injustices. Misery is misery, discontent is discontent, says the utilitarian, and from his point of view its etiology is of no great moment.[8] But utilitarianism, of course, is only incidentally if at all a member of the family of theories of justice. It is much more plausible to view utilitarianism as a substitute for a theory of justice, or as an attempt to supercede justice, and *a fortiori* not as a possible theory of social justice. Incorporating the factor of need into a genuine theory of justice in order to produce a theory of social justice is the real challenge. Utilitarians typically do not address that task and so their views do not qualify for further consideration in this context.

Historically, needs and social justice come into focus together in the socialism of the early nineteenth century. All three are epitomized in the slogan of the Gotha Program, borrowed from Louis Blanc and made famous in Karl Marx's critique, "From each according to his abilities, to each according to his needs."[9] (In passing we might note that intellectual historians of the future may well point to this slogan as the spiritual forefather of Rawls's Difference Principle, even though Rawls himself has not done so.[10]) This formulation is important for several reasons. One is that it is offered as a precept of justice, perhaps the first such to stress any role for need. Another reason is that unlike previous precepts of distributive justice, this one comes closer to suggesting a linkage between distribution and production. Abilities are what produces goods and services, which in turn can be used to satisfy needs, which in their turn give rise to new productivity and renewed abilities. The Gotha Program slogan, of course, no more than hints at this; still, it is on the way to replacing the static picture that the classic paradigms of distributive justice yield with a more dynamic one. The problem of distributive justice is *not* the one-time allocation of a fixed but divisible commodity among several claimants by means of some rule implemented by central authority. Whatever else social justice is, it requires the repudiation of such static paradigms of distribution and the simple-minded conceptions to which they give rise.

Not surprisingly, we can correlate the provisions of a theory of social justice with the development during the past century of the Welfare State. In particular, social justice, being addressed to the identification and satisfaction of basic human needs first and foremost, is the underlying rationale for the "safety net" that the "social minimum" provides.[11] (This, by the way, can be found also in Rawls, where in one of the very few places he explicitly discusses basic human needs, he directly connects them with the social minimum and indirectly with the Difference Principle.[12]) Classical theories of distributive justice do not provide a rationale for the social minimum because they cannot recognize any merit in claims based on needs, whereas it is precisely claims of this sort that generate both the rationale for and the content of the social minimum. Many of us (the more fortunate) do not have to rely on the social safety net to catch us, because we can support ourselves. Nevertheless, our needs do not go away nor do they get transformed; they remain relatively fixed across a broad range throughout our lives. The familiar contours of the Welfare State confront those needs only at a few points. The rest of our needs and their satisfaction must rely on other considerations, which will no doubt vary from society to society and epoch to epoch. It is one of the many merits of Rawls's theory of social justice that it goes farther than any other theory known to me to incorporate recognition of all our human needs into its basic principles. This is not the usual way in which Rawls's theory is interpreted; he himself shies away from doing so. Nevertheless, it could be argued (here, I can do no more than hint) that this may be the best way to link together his doctrine of primary goods, the original position, the principles of justice, their lexical order, and the constitutional democratic socialism that are such conspicuous features of his theory.

III

Recent (post-Rawlsian) non-utilitarian theories of justice characterize the status of needs in diverse and unsatisfactory ways. These theories can be divided roughly into three groups.

First, there are those whom I will call the *anti-need* theorists. Bruce Ackerman, in his recent book *Social Justice in the Liberal State* (1980), virtually ignores the concept of need altogether.[13] In this respect, his position is less like traditional conceptions of what we have come to understand by the "liberal state" and more like current libertarianism, such as can be found in the writings on justice of F. A. von Hayek, Robert Nozick, and more recently Richard Posner, whose book *Economic Justice* (1981) is a paean of praise to the doctrine that if only we would bend our efforts to maximize social wealth, all human needs will take care of themselves.[14] Why Ackerman regards his theory as a liberal theory of *social* justice is something of a mystery; no such puzzle presents itself in the writings of these other conservative libertarians because none professes to be offering a theory of *social* justice. The most that can be said on any of these theories so far as needs are concerned is that if they are to be taken into account at all, it must be done implicitly, indirectly, and contingently. Such a strategy challenges us to ask whether it is true, after all, that this is the best way to take some needs into account. That it is not the best way to take all basic human needs into account is an implicit thesis of every theory of social justice.

Second, there are those whom I will call the *quondam needs* theorists. Their theories do allow a sometime role for needs as such, except that it always seems to turn out that the claims based solely on need have such slight weight that they end up by determining the distribution or arrangement or structure of nothing. Thus, John Lucas in his recent book *On Justice* (1980) mentions need quite explicitly and more than once as a claim of justice, but he denies it pride of place among the classic rivals (desert, merit, agreements, work) for that role.[15] This is reminiscent of the views of Nicholas Rescher, who cited as a "canon of distributive justice" what he called "the canon of need," only to conclude that this canon has little or no weight.[16] David Miller, in his *Social Justice* (1976), a useful historical survey of the views on social justice of Hume, Spencer, and Kropotkin, cites a "principle of need" as one of three fundamentally conflicting interpretations of social justice. Unlike Lucas and Rescher, Miller thinks the needs principle is every bit as fundamental to justice as the desert and the rights principles, with which it is in chronic conceptual and empirical conflict. What he does not do is see any non-arbitrary way to resolve this conflict. Social justice, on Miller's view, remains hopelessly riven by the tensions introduced from these three directions simultaneously and independently.[17]

Finally, there are those whom I shall dub the *soi-disant needs* theorists, philosophers who explicitly stress the supremacy of needs in their theories of justice — only to leave the reader rather in the dark as to precisely how their theories really do accommodate needs in the end. Thus, William Galston insists in *Justice and Human Good* (1980) that the role of needs is paramount; accordingly, his "principle of need" dictates that "the primary basis of income distribution is *need*." This is crucial, because a person's income is the primary mode by means of which all possible objects of desire-, want-, and interest-satisfaction are brought within his reach. Increasing a person's income thus virtually guarantees enabling the person to increase his or her own ability to satisfy his or her own needs. But Galston's principle turns out to be somewhat half-hearted for at least three related reasons. First, he explicitly denies that this principle has lexical priority over other considerations. Also, he is silent on how incomes are to be matched up with needs so that his principle can be satisfied. For example, are salaried employees to get raises according to their needs? Is some central authority to be invested with the power and capacity to identify all the needs of all the members of the society and to allocate occupations and incomes from them according to need-satisfaction? We are left to guess. Finally, Galston nowhere indicates any structural or institutional features of the ideally just society that would show us how to give effect and stability to the principle of need.[18] James Sterba, in *The Demands of Justice* (1980), offers a doctrine of need-satisfaction less elaborate but with much the same features as Galston's; it is subject to the same criticisms.[19] Neither Galston nor Sterba calls his theory a theory of *social* justice. This does not matter, of course. What matters is that their theory gives human needs an explicit and prominent role in the factors that are identified as determining the principles of justice.

Soi-disant needs theorists I regard as co-workers struggling in the right direction. They can be viewed as attempting to remedy what they regard as the unsatisfactory way in which Rawls's liberal theory of social justice accomodates needs. In what follows I shall have no reason to refer further to their views. Instead, my remarks henceforth are aimed at the views of those with whom I regard myself most in disagreement, the anti-need theorists and to a less extent the *quondam* need theorists. It is their views that constitute the greatest challenge to the very idea of social justice. If they are right, an adequate theory of justice simply must take little or no direct account of human needs. Can such a view be correct?

It may be useful to focus directly on the kinds of considerations that can be brought to express that outlook. Here, succinctly, is a set of several possible reasons that emerge from the arguments of the anti-need and the *quondam* need theorists against incorporating considerations of need into the theory of justice:

(1) We don't know what a human need is.

(2) Insofar as we do, there is no rational basis for a distinction between genuine and spurious needs, between basic (or underived) and contingent (or cultivated) needs.

(3) Insofar as there is, the best way to make the distinction is individually

and subjectively, relying on the experience and judgment of each person whose needs are in question.

(4) Once that is done, there is no possible way for social institutions to take need-satisfaction directly into account.

(5) In any case, insofar as a person's needs make a moral claim on anyone else to satisfy them it is never a claim of justice — at best, it is a claim of charity.

(6) Insofar as it is more than that, other claims of justice invariably dominate claims based solely on needs.

(7) In any case, there is no way to arrange any society so as to satisfy everyone's needs, not even everyone's basic needs.

(8) Insofar as there is, it is best done indirectly and without deliberate intervention aimed at this end, by increasing the general level of productivity and consumption of all goods and services — in short, by maximizing wealth.

(9) Insofar as needs cannot be met in this way, nothing less than endless intervention and unlimited political power will be required in a futile effort to try to meet them.

(10) Insofar as social needs are concerned, they are identical with the needs that public goods satisfy, and such needs play no role in a theory of justice; their role is explained in the theory of public expenditure.

It would be a useful exercise to examine the merit of each of these reasons, but instead of undertaking this task here, I shall content myself with trying to offer a more constructive view of the nature and role of needs in the theory of justice. What I am about to say can be most directly connected with the foregoing list of propositions by viewing it as a partial criticism of proposition (5).

IV

From the start, I have insisted that the distinctive thing about a theory of social justice is that it incorporates some argument to the effect that a conception of justice that ignores needs is for that very reason a deficient theory. What, however, is really wrong about such a theory of justice? What's wrong, to put it as briefly as possible, is that it's *unfair* — and if it is unfair, then I cannot see any good reason for hesitating to go on to say that it is *unjust*. What I want to do now is to sketch the intuitive basis for such a judgment. Here is the core of the argument:

Let us begin by granting that there are needs of which it is true to say

(a) a person, A, has some needs he can't help having.

That is, A's needs are not cultivated but are natural or basic. Roughly, needs are basic to the extent that whatever else one wants or desires, these needs must be satisfied. Let us further grant that when (a) is true it is also sometimes true that

(b) person A is unable to meet (some or all of) these needs without being at fault for so failing.

For example, he can fall sick, or be abandoned in infancy, or be thrown out of work during a period of economic recession. In such circumstances A cannot be deemed to be at fault for being unable to satisfy the needs in question. (Contrast with this a person's being unable to meet his needs because he refused to eat the food available to him, or because he refused to take any of the jobs available, or because he insists on wasting his resources and energies. Proposition (b) does not apply to unsatisfied needs of this sort.)

Now, although needs and circumstances that make propositions (a) and (b) true can occur in social isolation, they cannot in that case give rise to claims of justice. The reason for supposing that (a) and (b) do give rise to claims of justice require two further assumptions of fact that involve other persons besides A, as follows:

(c) There are other persons, B, C, D,..., whose needs are met, who control a surplus of what would suffice to meet the needs of A, who are aware of A's plight, and who are in a position to meet A's needs.

(d) In the absence of transfers from B, C, D... (or some combination thereof, e.g., more from B to balance less from D) to A, A's needs will not be met.

As an example, think of a group of survivors in a lifeboat contemplating whether to help aboard another survivor still in the water, when there is no other life boat in sight, no life jacket to throw to the swimmer, and room and provisions aboard the boat adequate to accommodate another passenger. I claim that given (a), (b), (c), and (d), it is *unfair* of B, C, D... to leave A's needs unmet. And in this implication we have a paradigm of how the satisfaction of needs is to be acknowledged as a claim of justice. The task of a theory of social justice is to tell us the best way to take such needs into account and how to arrange to meet them. This, in effect, is to tell us how persons such as A, B, C, D... should arrange their affairs in advance against the day when any of them is in A's position.

In order to see the force and limitations of the foregoing argument, several comments on certain details are now in order.

First, the argument assumes that A, B, C, D... have the *same* needs, or at least, that the needs under discussion in this argument are the same needs. Special claims made by special needs that A has but B lacks are not covered by this argument. Whether it can be extended to cover such special needs is beyond my present purposes to examine. Notice, too, that the argument assumes no scarcity of the things sufficient to satisfy *all* the needs of A, B, C, D... It is not the quantity but the control of the need-satisfying things that accounts for the unfairness in leaving A's needs unmet.

Second, the argument does not rest on impugning the *entitlement* of B, C, D... to the surplus they control. Nothing so elaborate as a theory of social justice is needed to cope with cases where those who control goods and services are not entitled to do so because their control has been acquired through force or fraud. The purpose of the argument is to show that despite one's entitlement to a surplus, conditions can arise that make it unfair to refuse to part with it. The argument claims that, given (a) through (d), a failure or refusal to transfer some of that surplus is unfair *to* A and unfair *of* B, C, D...

Notice next that the argument does not rest on imputing to A any claim that any of the surplus is *due* or is *owed* to him because of his need. Some philosophers claim there is an important difference between (i) cases where denying someone something would be unfair, and (ii) cases where denying someone something would be denying him what he is owed or his due.[20] I am willing to grant this distinction, but I do not see any good reason for supposing that unfairness is morally less fundamental than failure to pay debts; nor do I see any good reason for tying injustice exclusively to the latter sort of act. To do that is to trivialize the role of justice in socio-economic and political life by narrowing its scope to the point where it cannot be what it ought to be, the first virtue of social life.

Some might claim that the judgment of unfairness depends on some tacit and *special moral relationship* that ties A to B, C, D.... Thus, every child, at least during much of its early life, satisfies the conditions in propositions (a) and (b), and most parents satisfy the conditions in propositions (c) and (d). When all this is true, surely it would be both unfair and unjust of the parents not to care for their children's needs, and not merely uncharitable and criminally negligent (though it would be these things, too). But my claim is that the injustice of parental neglect in cases of this sort does not arise from the special moral relation that we may suppose obtains between parents and their children. The parent-and-child case is merely one where we see quite clearly the unfairness in ignoring needs; it is a case where our sensibilities are most likely to be outraged, because at one time in our lives every one of us was in the position of the needy child. Yet I see no reason why the validity of the argument must turn on the existence of a special moral relation of this sort to be found between parents and their children.

Suppose that A, the child, in question, is *not* the child of B and C. Surely, it will not do to suppose that, with this alteration in the facts, the validity of the argument evaporates. Surely, it is quite as *unfair* of B and C to refuse to come to the aid of A, when A turns out not to be their own child, as it does when A is their child. (It may not be as wrong or as reprehensible, but that is another matter.) If that is granted, then there is no way to blunt the force of the argument for all possible combinations of persons, just so long as they satisfy the four premises (a) through (d). (Incidentally, it is worth noting in this connection that the inference to unfairness does not depend on even that attenuated but nonetheless genuine special moral relationship that Rawls to some extent relies upon, namely, the existence of a cooperative scheme of mutual participation for common goals.[21] To put the point another way, the argument's validity does not depend on a tacit premise alluding to the duty of fair play. If I am right, the argument applies in situations where A, B, C, D... are utter strangers.)

Further, the transfer from B, C, D... to A that is required by the argument need not be *voluntary*. That is, A may take what he needs from the others, without their permission and even despite their refusal, without being unfair to them in doing so. It would not be wrong or unjust or unfair, but fair, to force B, C, D... to aid A, even though they are in no way at fault for A's plight. It is central to the argument that each of A, B, C, D... is assumed not to be at fault for A's having the needs in the first place or for A's inability to satisfy them except by access to the surplus controlled by the others.

Finally, we may note that the account given here of needs in the argument stated above does not blur or contradict either the Kantian or the Christian doctrines that might at first seem to be at variance with it. My condition (b) is crucial though tacit to Kant's claim discussed earlier, that charity is a duty of imperfect obligation. If that condition is not satisfied, then it seems to me that Kant is right: The claims of the needy person against the other(s) who can meet those needs are not, or cannot without further ado be said to be, claims of justice. The modern interpretation of the Christian story of the Good Samaritan holds that by coming to the aid of the stranger in the ditch, the benefactor performs a supererogatory act, an act above and beyond the call of duty, and hence an act beyond what justice requires. Quite so, as long as it is not specified that my condition (c) holds. Otherwise, for all the Good Samaritan knows, he, too, may wind up in the ditch—and he will, if the thieves are still hidden and waiting to assault the next unwary passerby. Coming to the aid of a perfect stranger at the risk of one's own life and limb is a heroic act, something not required by justice. But this does not contradict the argument whose premises are (a) through (d) above.

V

The simplest way to view the connection among needs, the social minimum, and social justice is to see the argument discussed above as the paradigm for an argument that culminates in establishing institutions whose purpose is to ascertain basic human needs, to obtain the resources necessary to meet them, and then to arrange for the distribution of these resources. I do not, of course, suppose that the theory of social justice should be developed straightaway by taking the intuitive argument of the previous section and generalizing it step by step to cover an ever wider range of cases until the needs of everyone in every possible social situation are included. My purpose was merely to show the intuitive basis for incorporating need-satisfaction directly as a requirement of justice. Many complications enter the picture immediately once we move from the conditions defined strictly by propositions (a) through (d) to the larger setting of a whole society.

For one thing, there is a certain arbitrariness concerning the level at which society should aim to satisfy the needs in question. Quite apart from scarcity (which has been ignored in this entire discussion), it is arguable even in the paradigm case above what exactly should count as partial in contrast to full need-satisfaction. When one is concerned with institutions whose task it is to satisfy on a continuing basis the enduring needs of a whole society, it is probably too much to hope for more than rough justice. One's best hope is to set up stable institutions that operate fairly so that the particular allocations can be defended against general criticisms of injustice (what Rawls calls "pure procedural justice") and then adjusted or fine-tuned as a second approximation case by case so far as the standard equitable considerations allow.

For another, the distinction in the paradigm on which proposition (b) relies, between faultless and faulty inability to satisfy one's own basic needs, is roughly counterpart to the classic distinction of a century ago between the "deserving" and the "undeserving" poor. The Welfare State and the social minimum were originally designed to cater solely to the needs of the first. The entire argument of the paradigm relies on this.

In a modern society such as ours, with conditions of employment subject to a multitude of factors over which no one person has control, factors that reflect the overall state of the economy, the distinction between the deserving and the undeserving poor blurs and perhaps evaporates altogether. At least, at the level of institutions, it is more plausible to see those who are worst off as determined by some suitable standard, and therefore most in need of transfers of income, as occupying their status for systemic reasons rather than for reasons of culpable sloth, much less perverse preference, all of which are the favorite explanatory factors among conservatives and libertarians for the unmet needs of the needy.

Finally, once it is decided to respect what the economist calls "consumer sovereignty," by enabling the needy to satisfy their needs according to their own preferences, what gets put directly into their hands is not the goods and services that accomplish this, but money. Only purchasing power enables each needy person to decide what will be her or his schedule of need-satisfaction. As soon as this is done, the possibilities of irrationality and of abuse arise. The milder forms include the use of food stamps to buy steak and other edibles that are nutritionally unnecessary. The graver forms include the use of social security checks to buy alcohol and narcotics, thereby leaving genuine needs wholly unmet. It is hard to see what claim of justice in the latter sort of case a person would have against a system that denied him any further support. Yet it is also difficult to see what other social arrangement is preferable in a political economy such as ours to one that provides the social minimum to all adult persons, the prudent and the imprudent alike, in the form of money.

VI

Man, it has been said on good authority, does not live by bread alone. That is the biblical version of the truth that among the basic needs of all persons there are others besides the *material* needs to which alone the propositions in my earlier argument apply. What are these other needs and what has the theory of social justice to say about their satisfaction? I do not have space here to elaborate on the answer, but perhaps that is unnecessary. We already have a good sketch (indeed, the best I know of) in Rawls's theory. The first of his two principles of justice, the principle of greatest equal liberty, can be said to deal with the spiritual needs of persons, just as the other — the difference principle — deals with the material, with the two semi-separate domains bridged by the principle of fair equality of opportunity. These principles, as I remarked earlier, can be seen as an attempt to identify the governing ideas for the satisfaction of all our basic and continuing needs through the establishment of certain basic social institutions.

It does not matter whether you regard Rawls's theory of social justice as adequate in all respects. What does matter is whether you agree that it is the right *sort* of theory. I have argued that the distinctive trait of a theory of social justice is that it is designed to identify and explain how and why human needs should be satisfied. Classical theories of justice, beginning with Aristotle, are not aimed at that task. Modern theories of social justice are, or ought to be; it is the one distinctive task ignored, and even repudiated, by earlier philosophers. But only a suitably broad and deep appreciation of what human needs really are can suffice; otherwise the theory ends up coping with a misleadingly narrow range of problems. The task that remains for social philosophers during the rest of this century and beyond is to show in detail and against the fullest possible normative and empirical background just what all our needs are and the best way to provide for their satisfaction.

Tufts University

NOTES

1. W. I. Matson, "What Rawls Calls Justice," *The Occasional Review*, 8/9 (Autumn 1978), p. 55.

2. See A. M. Honore, "Social Justice," in R. S. Summers, ed., *Essays in Legal Philosophy* (Blackwells, 1971), p. 61, and David Miller, *Social Justice* (Oxford, 1976), p. 23.

3. *Op. cit.*, note 2.

4. F. A. von Hayek, *The Mirage of Social Justice* (Chicago, 1976), p. 63. Cf. W. T. Blackstone and R. D. Heslep, eds., *Social Justice and Preferential Treatment* (Georgia, 1977), p. ix; W. Lang, "Marxism, Liberalism, and Justice," in E. Kamenka and A. E.-S. Tay, eds., *Justice* (Arnold, 1979), pp. 129, 133; W. A. Galston, *Justice and the Human Good* (Chicago, 1980), p. 113.

5. John Rawls, *A Theory of Justice* (Harvard, 1971), pp. 4, 7. The term 'social justice,' however does not appear in his index nor in his table of contents, it is not, in other words, a term of art in his lexicon.

6. A critic who does is T. L. Beauchamp, "Distributive Justice and the Difference Principle," in H. G. Blocker and E. H. Smith, eds., *John Rawls' Theory of Social Justice* (Ohio, 1980), pp. 132-61.

7. I. Kant, *The Fundamental Principles of the Metaphysics of Morals* (tr. L. W. Beck; Bobbs-Merrill, 1959), p. 39.

8. This is not Mill's view, however. He preserves exactly Kant's contrast between duties of justice and other moral duties (see his *Utilitarianism*, part five, paragraph fifteen). Although Mill seems to ignore the point, his view entails that he should accord greater moral weight to the distress from unrequited desert than to the distress from unmet needs, however trivial the dessert and urgent the need.

9. Karl Marx, "Critique of the Gotha Program," in *Basic Writings on Politics and Philosophy: Karl Marx and Friedrich Engels* (ed. L. W. Feuer; Anchor, 1959), p. 119. W. G. Runciman, *Relative Deprivation and Social Justice* (Routledge & Kegan Paul, 1966), p. 266, alleges that this idea goes back a century and more earlier to the *philosophes*.

10. Rawls, *op. cit.*, p. 305, mentions this slogan but essentially ignores it as a "precept of justice" of no great interest.

11. See Runciman, *op. cit.*, pp. 70, 77f., 268. One of the earliest and most influential developments in this direction among English speaking thinkers is to be found in L. T. Hobhouse, *The Elements of Social Justice* (Holt, 1922). J. A. Passmore, "Civil Justice and its Rivals," in Kamenka and Tay, *op. cit.*, pp. 35-47, argues that social justice (he identifies several varieties) is always addressed to "disadvantages." This is not my view; having a need is not, in general, having a disadvantage.

12. Rawls, *op. cit.*, p. 276.

13. B. A. Ackerman, *Social Justice in the Liberal State* (Yale, 1980), treats of needs only in the sense of special needs (e.g., of the physically handicapped); his discussion of wealth (pp. 31-68) proceeds without any explicit reference to anyone's needs.

14. R. A. Posner, *The Economics of Justice* (Harvard, 1981), mentions needs in passing (pp. 68, 81) but explicitly disregards any attempt to formulate any requirements of justice in its terms.

15. J. R. Lucas, *On Justice* (Clarendon Press, 1980), pp. 164-70.

16. N. Rescher, *Distributive Justice* (Bobbs-Merrill, 1966), pp. 75-76.

17. Miller, *op. cit.*, pp. 27-28, 341-43.

18. Galston, *op. cit.*, pp. 162-70, 197-200, 223-24.

19. J. P. Sterba, *The Demands of Justice* (Notre Dame, 1980), pp. 51-56, 61.

20. Matson, *op. cit.*, p. 54.

21. Rawls, *op. cit.*, pp. 7, 16, 111-13, 126.

JUSTICE, EPISTEMOLOGY, AND ETHICAL COMPROMISE

Andrew Altman

One of the traditional tasks undertaken by ethical philosophers is that of deriving a set of ethical principles from premises that do not contain any controversial assumptions. What makes this task an important one, from a social as well as a philosophical perspective, is the existence of widespread ethical disagreement. Within our Western cultural tradition, and certainly between it and other traditions, one finds serious disagreements concerning questions about how individuals should lead their lives and arrange their social institutions. Philosophers who seek to derive ethical principles from noncontroversial premises do so in the hope that they may succeed in resolving such disagreements.

Among the most controversial of ethical disputes are those concerning social justice. Such disputes are clearly serious ones when the parties belong to the same society, for they can undermine the trust and cooperation that underlie any social order. Yet, these disputes are also extremely serious when the parties belong to different societies, for it must not be forgotten that our current world is one of global interdependence in which multinational and international institutions play a very powerful role. Disagreements over how such institutions should operate in order to meet the demands of justice are among the most significant of our time. A philosophical theory of justice which derives normative principles from noncontroversial premises could, it seems, serve the important practical aim of generating a consensus out of intra- and international disagreements regarding social justice. In addition, such theories could seemingly serve the philosophical purpose of rationally justifying a set of principles of social justice.

Nonetheless, against this rather sanguine view of the possibilities of a philosophical theory of justice, I shall argue that the task of deriving a set of ethical principles from noncontroversial premises rests upon a highly dubious epistemological assumption. When that assumption is rejected, a persuasive case can be made that the task is a futile one and can achieve neither its practical nor its philosophical aim. In short, irresolvable disagreement over the questions of social jusice is a fact of human life. This does not entail, however, that philosophers must resign themselves to the idea that coercion and violence are the only ways in which such disagreements can be handled. I shall argue that intelligence can be used to effect peaceful and voluntary settlements of at least some such disagreements, although not by deriving principles that all parties would accept as the correct ones. Rather, intelligence can be used in the development of practical compromises which parties to the disagreement could voluntarily live with, though they would not accept any such arrangement as fully embodying what they conceive of as the correct principles of social justice.

My argument against the epistemological assumption behind the attempted derivation of ethical principles from noncontroversial assumptions is based upon a position associated with Duhem and Quine. In the next section, I shall argue that if the Duhem-Quine position can be legitimately applied to ethical beliefs, then such derivations can achieve neither their practical nor their philosophical aim. In section III, I shall argue that the Duhem-Quine position can be legitimately applied to ethical beliefs. Section IV will explain my view that philosophers should assist in resolving ethical disagreements by helping to work out practical compromises and will contain a limited defense of that view.

II

The notion that principles of justice should be derived from noncontroversial premises is not an arbitrary one. It follows from a traditional conception of justification according to which a controverted ethical statement can be justified in a non-question begging fashion only by deducing it from premises that any rational person would accept, no matter what his initial ethical viewpoint. The justification of principles of justice is thus thought to require the formulation of a sound deductive argument with the principles as the conclusion and only statements which no rational person would dispute as the premises. In short, justifying such principles is justifying them to all possible rational individuals, given this traditional conception.[1]

In the attempt to deduce ethical principles from noncontroversial assumptions, philosophers have adopted one of two basic strategies. On the first, the derivation proceeds from premises that purportedly contain no substantive ethical judgments.[2] Typically the premises will contain claims regarding the concept of action, the principles of practical rationality, the nature of personhood, human nature and the like. Recent examples of such theories are found in the work of Gewirth, Gert and Brandt.[3] On the second strategy, substantive ethical claims are included among the premises, although, of course, it is alleged or assumed that they are noncontroversial.

The original position argument expounded by Rawls in *A Theory of Justice* can be interpreted as an example of this second strategy.[4]

An epistemological position formulated by Duhem and later generalized by Quine renders dubious the attempt to justify ethical principles, including principles of justice, by either of the two strategies. Duhem argued that with regard to the theories of physics there was no such thing as a crucial experiment.[5] An experiment whose outcome contradicted some principle of a given physical theory did not rationally compel the scientist to reject the principle. Duhem pointed out that a conjunction of several statements was always required to derive the contradiction of a given physical principle, and the scientist always had the option of judging that some other statement in the conjunction was less credible than the principle under test. In that way, he could continue to accept the principle in the face of apparent disconfirmation. Of course, it was also open to any individual scientist to accept the other statements and reject the principle. Duhem's point was that epistemic rationality left open the question of whether the principle or some other statement should be discarded.

Quine generalized Duhem's point by viewing each person's entire corpus of beliefs about physical objects as a kind of scientific theory.[6] Whenever the individual came up against some experience that apparently contradicted some such belief, there were a number of options open to him on how to adjust his corpus to render it consistent with the experience. He could, for example, continue to accept the belief which appeared to be contradicted and construe the experience as hallucinatory; or he could count the experience as veridical and reject the belief in question. Epistemic rationality required that some adjustment in an individual's corpus be made when he faced a recalcitrant experience, and that certain broad criteria such as simplicity and generality be utilized in determining what adjustments to make;[7] but it did not specify any particular beliefs that had to be accepted nor any particular ones that had to be rejected.

It is not my intention to defend the Duhem-Quine position in this paper. Such a defense would take us into the far reaches of epistemology and semantics, and the reader can refer to the work of Quine, who has defended the position cogently. What I shall do is to apply the Duhem-Quine position to ethical beliefs. Quine himself did not do this, perhaps thinking that ethical beliefs were epistemically suspect in a way beliefs about physical objects were not and so should be evicted en masse from our total corpus of belief. If this was Quine's thinking, in the next section, I shall try to put such doubts regarding ethical beliefs to rest. In this section, I shall simply assume that ethical beliefs are legitimate members of our corpus.

Once ethical beliefs are so acknowledged, the Duhem-Quine position can serve as the basis for an argument critical of the attempt to derive principles of justice from noncontroversial premises. In order to see this, let us envision a disagreement over the correct principles of social justice. One party asserts that P_1 is the correct principle; the other asserts that it is some conflicting principle, P_2. The disputants could be Rawls and Nozick, Bentham and Dworkin, or Kennedy and Reagan. The precise content of the principles under dispute is irrelevant here. Now suppose that a valid derivation of P_1 is formulated from premises A, B, C...J. If the Duhem-Quine position is sound, then there is no constraint of epistemic rationality that requires the proponent of P_2 to place greater credence in the conjunction of A...J than in P_2 itself. He could, consistent with the demands of rationality, place greater initial credence in P_2 than in that conjunction, or in any given conjunct taken individually, and in doing so reject the derivation as unsound. This is true independent of the content of the premises, A...J, and independent of the content of the principle, P_2. The dubious epistemological assumption behind the attempt to generate a unique rational resolution of ethical disagreements by means of such derivations is that there is some privileged set of premises which are inherently more credible than any of the principles over which the disagreement takes place. In other words, it is assumed that there is some special set of premises which epistemic rationality requires all of us to give greater credence to than that given to any of the principles under dispute.[8] Given the Duhem-Quine position, this assumption is untenable: there simply is no set of inherently noncontroversial premises.

If my argument is sound to this point, it follows that no derivation of any set of principles of justice can satisfy the traditional conception of justification. It is always possible for a rational individual to reject the premises of any derivation as inconsistent with an ethical belief to which he attaches greater credence. Yet, it is precisely such a possibility that any sound justification argument must rule out, given the traditional conception. I conclude, then, that the logical derivation of principles of justice cannot succeed in satisfying the requirements of the traditional conception of justification.[9]

This still leaves open the question of whether some derivation or other can achieve the practical aim of generating consensus out of disagreement on matters of social justice. For it is still possible that some derivation could generate (near) universal, de facto agreement, even though it is also true that an individual *would* not be irrational *were* he to reject the derivation and place greater credence in some conflicting set of principles. However, I believe that once a commonly recognized psychological truth is acknowledged, it will become clear that the practical aim is very unlikely to be fulfilled.

It will be generally acknowledged that questions regarding social justice are ones about which individuals have extremely strong and unyielding convictions. On the other hand, beliefs about personhood, practical rationality and the like are ones about which convictions are decidedly less strong. Any derivation whose premises include claims about such matters and whose conclusion contradicts the initial beliefs of an individual regarding justice is likely to be rejected by him, for the initial credence he attaches to his beliefs about justice will be much greater than that which he attaches to the premises. Yet, any derivation which hopes to generate consensus out of discord will have to persuade many individuals to accept its premises as more credible than their beliefs about justice. This may not be impossible, but a realistic understanding of the psychology of the situation argues for the conclusion that it is extremely unlikely.[10] Moreover, even if principles of justice were derived from an overarching ethical principle which all parties to the dispute in fact accepted there would still be a problem in generating consensus. The individuals whose initial beliefs about justice were contradicted by the derivation would still have several options other than jettisoning those beliefs and accepting the conclusion of the derivation. They could, of course, reject the overarching ethical principle that serves as the premise, but, more likely, they could simply interpret the principle so that it did not apply to the matter under dispute. This is precisely how the apologists for Black slavery reconciled their Christian ethical principles with their endorsement of such slavery: the ethical principles constraining our behavior with regard to human beings simply did not apply to relations with Blacks, in their view. The fact that abolitionists and apologists accepted the same Christian principles did not help to generate any consensus among them, for the principles were applied in different ways. In brief, then, given the strength of convictions regarding social justice and given the manifold options which an individual has other than giving up those beliefs when faced with some philosophical derivation of contrary ones, it is highly unlikely that such derivations can fulfill the practical aim of generating consensus out of disagreement.

III

My assumption that ethical beliefs are bona fide members of our corpus, meriting as a class no special epistemic suspicion, might be challenged in the following manner. Beliefs regarding rabbits, brick houses, protons and the like all make contact, even if only indirectly, with observational experience. They are testable and revisable in the light of such experience. Yet, beliefs regarding justice and other ethical matters appear prima facie to be incapable of any kind of observational testing, even a highly indirect one. On these grounds, it might be argued that beliefs regarding justice and other ethical matters should be expelled from our corpus and re-admitted if and only if it can be shown that these beliefs are in some way derivable from a class of beliefs that do have observational consequences.

This basic line of argument against my view needs to be filled out with an analysis of the nature of observation and observational testing, and there are undoubtedly several ways in which this might be done. For current purposes, I shall examine the position of the contemporary philosopher who has faced most directly this issue of the observational import of ethical beliefs and who has sought to fill out precisely that line of argument against my view described in the previous paragraph, viz., Gilbert Harman.[11] In what follows, I shall attempt to refute Harman's argument that ethical beliefs as a class are epistemically suspect in a way beliefs about rabbits, protons, etc. are not. I should mention in passing that Harman does eventually re-certify ethical beliefs as bona fide members of our corpus, but only after he has argued that they are reducible to a class of beliefs which he takes from the start to be bona fide. My disagreement with Harman is over his thesis that ethical beliefs are suspect to begin with and need to be reduced to another class of beliefs in order to regain their epistemic credentials.

Harman begins his argument by claiming that, although there are ethical observations, they do not appear to permit the observational testing of ethical beliefs that would immediately certify such beliefs as legitimate members of our corpus. That there are ethical observations is due to two facts: (1) what an individual perceives is a function of the general background theory of the world that he holds, and (2) some ethical theory is part of nearly every individual's background theory. Individuals perceive the rightness and wrongness of actions and institutions in the same way they perceive certain entities as particular kinds of mind-independent objects existing in space and time. Just as certain stimuli cause an individual to see things as houses, rabbits, etc., other stimuli cause the individual to see actions as right or wrong, just or unjust.[12]

Nonetheless, this does not entail that ethical beliefs can be supported by observational testing, claims Harman. In his view, such support requires that the *truth* of a belief be usable to help give a reasonable explanation of

why certain observations are made. Now, the truth of the belief that protons exist can be used to help give a reasonable explanation of why the
physicist sees tracks in his cloud chamber. However, Harman suggests that
the truth of ethical beliefs does not appear to help explain any observations,
including ethical ones. What explains why Joe perceived the murder he
witnessed as wrong is not the truth of the ethical belief that murder is
wrong, but rather the truth of the factual belief that Joe thinks murder is
wrong. In general, psychological truths about what individuals believe, not
ethical truths, explain their ethical observations. Harman concludes that
ethical beliefs are prima facie suspect and need to be reduced to some
respectable class of beliefs in order to regain their epistemic credentials.[13]

Harman's argument is guilty of a question-begging bias against ethical
beliefs. He takes it for granted that, while some physical object beliefs can
be assumed to be justified, no ethical beliefs can be so assumed. In order to
see this clearly, it is important to recognize that not only is observation
theory-laden, but explanation is so as well. What an individual will count as
a reasonable explanation is a function of what background beliefs he takes
to be justified. If we begin by doubting the justifiability of some class of
beliefs, such as those regarding physical objects or those regarding moral
right or wrong, then that very fact will bar us from invoking the truth of any
beliefs in the suspect class when offering explanations of phenomena to be
explained. Harman's example shows that he is not treating beliefs about
physical objects in that way. Some such beliefs are assumed, at the start, as
justified: the belief that this is a cloud-chamber, that it is filled with liquid,
that this is a vapor track, etc. Given that some such beliefs are initially
regarded as justified, no general problem arises when invoking the truth of
another physical object belief to explain the perceptions in question. Suppose, however, one were to adopt the stand of a skeptic regarding the
physical world and to begin inquiry by doubting the justifiability of all
beliefs about physical objects. Only beliefs about mental states would be
assumed to be justified. In such a case, the explanation that would be offered of a person's perceptions of a mind-independent physical world would
not be that there actually is such a world, but rather it would be that we
think that there is one (due to the force of some mental habit or some
philosophical confusion, e.g.). Locke's epistemological assumptions lead to
Hume's skepticism and Berkeley's idealism.

It is the attitude of the skeptic that Harman is adopting for ethical
beliefs, though rejecting for physical object beliefs. It is no mystery, then,
why ethical beliefs come off as epistemically suspect, while physical object
beliefs retain their epistemic credentials. For Harman is starting with the

assumption that, of the two classes of belief, only the latter can be assumed to be justified. If, to the contrary, we assume that some ethical beliefs are justified, then no general problem arises when invoking their truth to explain various phenomena. Anyone who thinks that he is justified in holding some ethical beliefs or other can reasonably invoke their truth in offering explanations of his own beliefs, perceptions and actions, as well as those of other individuals. Only if an individual doubts the justifiability of all ethical beliefs to begin with, will he refuse to invoke ethical truth in any of his explanations, and it is because of this that Harman's argument is question-begging.

IV

I have argued that epistemic rationality leaves many ethical disagreements as rationally irresolvable. This conclusion is liable to be of concern to philosophers who fear that it is tantamount to acquiescing in the use of force or violence to settle those disagreements. Such is far from the case, however. It should be recognized that no one need relinquish his conviction that violence and coercion are so undesirable as to make the resort to them, in many cases, ethically unjustifiable. Moreover, I believe that philosophers can assist in settling disagreements in a peaceful, non-coercive way if they take seriously the notion of ethical compromise. With regard to matters of social justice, the aim of developing such compromises would *not* be to generate some position that is believed to incorporate fully the correct principles of justice. Rather, it would be to generate some position the institutional embodiment of which all the parties to the dispute could voluntarily accept, although each would find it lacking in some respect when measured up against his own conception of the demands of justice.

It might be thought that such compromises would be consistent only with a teleological theory of justice, since practical compromises are presumably to be justified by their desirable outcomes. However, the fact is that even a rigidly deontological theory is consistent with accepting practical compromise as justifiable in at least some cases. This can be seen by considering Nozick's account of justice, which explicitly and forcefully repudiates any goal-directed conception of justice.

Nozick argues that individuals possess certain moral rights which are to be conceived as side-constraints in that violating such rights is always unjust no matter what goals might be advanced by doing so.[14] Since any practical compromise that might be proposed to a Nozickean would involve some rights violation (otherwise it would not be a compromise from the

Nozickean viewpoint), it appears that he would automatically rule it out as unacceptable. In this case, however, appearances are deceiving. It is crucial to distinguish between what an individual judges as fully just and what he can voluntarily accept, and even support, although he recognizes it to be, to some extent, unjust. A Nozickean *cannot* consistently maintain that a certain policy both violates rights and is just. However, a Nozickean *can* consistently reason that a certain policy, although it is unjust because it involves some rights violations, is the best that one can reasonably expect to see enacted at this time and so is deserving of support.

The side-constraints theory does not condemn the Nozickean to the futile position of having to support only those policies, platforms, etc., that coincide exactly with its rigorous demands of justice. If I am correct in this matter, then even a rigid deontological theory would not by itself be any bar to an individual who holds it accepting, and even supporting, a practical compromise which in some ways falls short of completely satisfying the principles of the theory.

It will be argued, however, that it is simply unreasonable to expect that persons will in fact compromise on issues of social justice for the same reason it is unreasonable to expect that they will reach a consensus on such issues, viz., that the convictions of individuals in this regard are strong and unyielding. Without downplaying the obstacle to compromise that is posed by such unyielding convicitons, it is important to recognize that the compromise approach I have suggested does not expect persons to relinquish their beliefs about justice, as does the consensus approach. Moreover, I believe that in many conflict situations there is some practical compromise whose outcome will be judged superior by the standards of each party to the dispute than the outcome that ensues from failing to reach any compromise at all. The approach which I suggest does expect that persons can recognize when practical compromise will yield an outcome that is superior, by their own standards, to that of the no compromise situation and can act without *akrasia* upon such a recognition. I believe that such an expectation is far more realistic than the one that underlies the consensus-building approach.

By way of clarifying the approach I am recommending, let me enumerate and briefly comment upon four theses which are consistent with it and all of which I would endorse.

(1) Compromise is not always ethically desirable.

My approach presupposes that compromise is sometimes desirable and should be pursued in those cases. It does not presuppose that it is always desirable.

(2) Philosophers should not relinquish their personal beliefs about social justice.

For philosophers to assist in constructing viable compromises, it is not incumbent upon them to relinquish their personal beliefs. As I have argued, practical compromise does not mean abandoning one's ethical beliefs.

(3) Philosophers can legitimately support the particular sides in controversies regarding social justice on which they happen to find themselves.

I am not suggesting that philosophers fight less vigorously for what they believe. I am suggesting that, to the extent that an individual undertakes philosophical thinking about ethics with the hope of helping to resolve intelligently cultural disputes about right and wrong, he should devote some of his energies to tasks that will assist in the construction of practical compromises which the parties to the disputes could voluntarily live with.

(4) Philosophers should not give up their attempts at developing normative theories of justice and of right.

Normative theories can help systematize a body of diverse beliefs. They can show which are relatively fundamental and which are derivative. They can display the logical links among the beliefs and provide a rationale for what is initially just intuitively held. To the extent a normative theory does these things, it can clarify and deepen the ethical thinking of the philosopher who constructs it and those in the culture who share his convictions. It can illuminate their ethical dilemmas and make more meaningful their ethical lives. In addition, it has the effect of assisting the possibility of compromise, for successful compromise is difficult if the individuals involved lack a clear conception of what they are aiming for and why. For these reasons, normative theory construction remains a valuable endeavor. Nonetheless, it must be stripped of the futile aim of developing a theory that can be justified to all rational individuals.

Practical compromise is no panacea for the evils that ensue when force and violence are utilized to settle conflicts over justice and right. There is no such panacea. Yet, the approach it represents does offer some realistic hope of reducing those evils. Historically committed to the use of human intelligence to resolve ethical disagreements, philosophers should take such an approach seriously.[15]

Indiana University of Pennsylvania

NOTES

1. The proper analysis of 'rational' in this context is a matter of some dispute, and I shall present my own views on the subject in the subsequent section. The point here is that, although philosophers who are committed to this traditional view of justification may disagree over the correct analysis of 'rational,' all of them agree that justification involves producing an argument acceptable to all possible rational minds.

2. As I am using the term, a substantive ethical judgment must be neither tautologous nor analytic.

3. Alan Gewirth, *Reason and Morality* (Chicago: University of Chicago Press, 1978); Bernard Gert, *The Moral Rules* (New York: Harper Torchbooks, 1973); Richard Brandt, *A Theory of the Good and the Right* (New York: Oxford, 1979).

4. One major criticism of the original position argument to be found in the literature is that it does in fact embody controversial ethical assumptions. See, e.g., Adina Schwartz, "Moral Neutrality and Primary Goods," *Ethics* LXXXIII: 4 (July 1973), 294-307.

5. Pierre Duhem, *The Aim and Structure of Physical Theory*, trans. by P. P. Wiener (Princeton: Princeton University Press, 1954), Chap. VI.

6. W. V. O. Quine, "Two Dogmas of Empiricism," in *From a Logical Point of View* (New York: Harper Torchbooks, 1963), pp. 42-46.

7. Quine and J. S. Ullian, *The Web of Belief*, second edition (New York: Random House, 1978), pp. 66-82.

8. The view I am criticizing here does *not necessarily* assume that the special premises are incorrigible.

9. I consider this to be grounds for accepting a different conception of justification, whose requirements can be satisfied, but for present purposes, it is not important that I spell out such a conception. For a different argument that concurs in my conclusion that no unique theory of justice can be rationally validated, see Adina Schwartz. "Against Universality," *Journal of Philosophy* LXXVIII: 3 (March 1981), 127-43. For my preferred conception of justification, see my "Pragmatism and Applied Ethics," *American Philosophical Quarterly*, forthcoming.

10. This is, I think, a principal weakness in the new methodology adopted by Rawls in his Dewey Lectures. There he conceives of the aim of his theory of justice to be that of generating a consensus in our culture on how institutions should, in order to meet the demands of justice, embody the values of liberty and equality. Rawls recognizes the disagreements which have existed, and continue to exist, over those values and hopes to resolve them by invoking a certain conception of personhood. My point is that it is much more likely that individuals who initially disagree with Rawls' conception of what justice demands would reject (or alter) the conception of personhood from which it derives than that they would give up their beliefs about justice. See "Kantian Constructivism in Moral Theory: The Dewey Lectures 1980," *Journal of Philosophy* LXXVII: 9 (September 1980).

11. Gilbert Harman, *The Nature of Morality* (New York: Oxford, 1977).

12. *Ibid.*, pp. 4-6.

13. *Ibid.*, pp. 6-10.

14. Robert Nozick. *Anarchy, State and Utopia* (New York: Basic Books, 1974), pp. 28-33.

15. As far as I know, there is at present only one piece in the philosophical literature that attempts to forge a viable compromise on a contentious issue involving social justice. See George Sher, "Subsidized Abortion: Moral Rights and Moral Compromise," *Philosophy and Public Affairs* 10: 4 (Fall 1981), 361-72. For general philosophical discussions of compromise and its desirability see Martin P. Golding, "The Nature of Compromise: A Preliminary Inquiry," *Nomos XXI: Compromise in Ethics, Law and Politics*, J. R. Pennock and J. Chapman, eds., (New York: New York University Press, 1979), pp. 3-25; and Arthur Kuflik, "Morality and Compromise," also in *Nomos XXI*, pp. 38-65.

LAW, MORALITY, AND OUR PSYCHOLOGICAL NATURE*

Laurence Thomas

> Le difficile est de ne promulguer que des lois
> nécessaires, de rester à jamais fidèle à ce principe
> vraiment constitutionnel de la société, de se mettre en
> garde contre la fureur de gouverner, la plus funeste
> maladie des gouvernments modernes.
>
> Mirabeau l'aîné, *Sur l'éducation publique*, p. 69

There are those who believe that their conception of the good life should be reflected in the basic structure of society; and there are those who believe that people should be free to pursue their own conception of the good, so long as they do not harm others. Both of these claims admit of further refinement, but I shall assume that the point being made here is well understood. I shall call the former conservatives and the latter liberals or social libertarians.[1] Members of the moral majority are a paradigm example of a conservative group. They believe not only that you, I, and everyone else should live according to the precepts of Christianity, but that the laws of society should not give the members of society too much latitude to live differently. Thus, because they deem pornographic entertainment to be contrary to these precepts, they hold both that individuals should not entertain themselves in this way and that the operation of all businesses which make pornographic entertainment possible should be illegal.

In this essay, I want to offer an argument against conservativism and for social libertarianism or liberalism, which comes to more than just declaring that diversity of lifestyles is a good in and of itself. For, while this claim (about lifestyles) may be true, conservative groups such as the moral majority stand as a reminder that it is not self-evidently true and, therefore, that an argument in support of it needs to be supplied. I shall attempt to ground my defense of liberalism in facts about our human nature. The argument which I shall make is not, I think, new with me. Something like it can be found in or, at any rate, is suggested by the writings of J. S. Mill.[2] My contribution shall be to make the argument more explicit, especially the premises about our human nature. The principal claims of the argument are as follows. 1) Throughout life, it is of fundamental importance that persons have a measure of psychological security which is in no way tied to approval on the part of others of their performances. I shall refer to this kind of psycholoical security as basic. 2) In the child, basic psychological security is engendered and sustained by parental love. 3) The social institutions of society are conducive to the adult members of society having basic psychological security if and only if such institutions are conducive to the members of society having the conviction that they have full moral status in virtue of being a person, and so their having the conviction that morality requires that they should not be treated in an arbitrary and capricious manner. As I shall understand it, having self-respect consists in having this conviction.[3] Social institutions which are supportive of the self-respect of persons are, I want to say, the social analogue to parental love. If this seems wildly implausible, let me just note that in so contending I suppose the truth of the preceding claims only. I do not suppose that the adult members of society must feel loved or some such thing by society's social institutions.

I

To bring into sharper focus the objective of this essay, I ask you to imagine a perfectly homogeneous society, which we may call Perfect Agreement Land or PAL for short. Everyone in PAL subscribes to the same set of values, and everyone knows that everyone does. And while everyone in PAL would strongly disapprove of anyone whose lifestyle does not reflect their shared values and would be inclined to disassociate himself from that person, such a person would not suffer from any institutional discrimination. A deviant in PAL could very well find himself without any friends; but from the standpoint of the rights, privileges, and liberties that are due to him as a citizen of good standing in PAL, he would never have to worry about being shortchanged. The intuitive idea here is this. When it comes to what is called criminal behavior, precious little is regarded as such if it is not contrary to what H. L. A. Hart calls the minimum content of law.[4] This conception refers to those laws which make possible the very existence of a stable society, such as laws against assault and battery, theft, and murder. So, almost any contractual arrangement or other activity between freely consenting adults is permitted. Hence, in PAL the criminal law is silent on virtually all sexual behavior between freely consenting adults. Persons in PAL whose behavior satisfies the minimum content of law are regarded as minimally good citizens; and from the standpoint of the social institutions of PAL all minimally good citizens are treated the same.

In view of the fact that only the most inured and strong willed among us, if any, would have the strength of character to endure such overwhelming disapproval of our lives, should we find ourselves the only deviant in PAL, it is obvious that life in PAL could be miserable. But things could be worse.

For, imagine another society just like PAL except that in this one the unanimously shared values are all enshrined in law. Strict PAL is the name of this society. In both PAL and Strict PAL, everyone disapproves of, for example, anyone's not going to church on Sunday (since everyone in the two societies subscribes to the Christian faith), but only in Strict PAL are there legal sanctions against not doing so. Only in the latter does not going to church constitute criminal behavior. Indeed, in Strict PAL the grounds for designating this or that lifestyle or behavior as criminal is just that everyone disapproves of it. So, there is not even the presumption that things which are designated as criminal are, or at least come close, to being contrary to the minimum content of law, whereas this presumption does hold in PAL.

As I have already noted, perhaps much can be said against PAL. Yet, I doubt that one can object on moral grounds. For morality does not require that someone or the other associate with us or approve of what we do. This is not to say that friendship is beyond the purview of morality. That is certainly false.[5] Rather, the point is that no one has a moral claim to our being her friend. This is so even if, as we may suppose is the case in PAL, our conception of morality calls for a great many positive duties on our part. After all, from the fact that morality may require us to aid someone whose life is in jeopardy, it does not follow that it requires us to be her friend or to approve of what she does. Anyway, there is no reason to think that even in a just society, one never has to pay a price for striking out on one's own. PAL reminds us that sometimes the price can be quite dear, if worth paying at all. As should be obvious from these remarks, I assume that PAL is not at odds with the demands of liberalism or, at any rate, a variety of it. We may think of a maximally liberal society as one whose social institutions encourage diversity of lifestyles and a minimally liberal society as one whose social institutions neither encourage nor discourage such diversity. PAL is a minimally liberal society. I shall not consider whether morality requires a maximally liberal society; for if morality does, then it will certainly follow that a minimally liberal one is superior to a conservative one, since maximal liberalism entails minimal liberalism. And my objective in this essay is just to show that minimal liberalism is morally superior to conservativism. For it will be remembered that my aim is to give an argument against conservativism and for liberalism. Throughout the remainder of this essay it is to be understood that I mean minimal liberalism.

(It is worth noting that while I have assumed that there is nothing morally objectionable about PAL, what matters is not so much that this is true, but that, in any case, Strict PAL is *more* morally objectionable than PAL. So, the assumption is quite innocuous.)

Turning to Strict PAL, it goes without saying that I take it to be a conservative society. And since my aim is to show that liberalism or social libertarianism is morally superior to conservativism, then it follows that I take the move from PAL to Strict PAL, by way of legislation which enshrines the values of the former into law, to be morally objectionable. But how can this be? After all, Strict PAL has no social institutions, such as the Nazi regime or American slavery, which are typically nefarious. No identifiable group of persons are targeted or discriminated against. It is true that a deviant in Strict PAL could easily find himself without a friend. But, as we have seen, PAL is hardly a haven for such persons. On what grounds, then, can it be said that Strict PAL is morally objectionable, but PAL is not? I attempt to answer this question in what follows. To this end, it will help to look briefly at the role which love plays in child development. For contrary to the way in which virtually all political and moral philosophy proceeds, we do not start in the world as fully developed individuals, ready to take our place in it. Nor, when it comes to the deep facts about human needs, does the transition from childhood to adulthood mark a radical change in our human nature. Accordingly, I believe that we can look with profit at the role which love plays in child development, as I trust will become evident as we proceed.

II

Simply put, love is that favorable attitude that we have toward persons, which is not conceptually tied to approval of their performances, although it involves considerable concern for their well-being and identification with their interests. Love is unconditional in that there are no beliefs concerning a person's behavior which constitute a conceptual bar to loving him.[6] Hence, there is no conceptual bar to loving one's enemy, however difficult that may be to do. It is, then, possible to love a person and disapprove of her or his behavior. Thus, love is quite distinct from praise, which is conceptually tied to a person's performances, since it is a form of approval. Praise which is not an expression of approval is empty and disingenuous, and necessarily so.

Now, it would appear to be an indisputable fact that parental love is indispensable to the psychological well-being of the child.[7] In view of the fact that love is not tied to an evaluation of a person's performances, it should be easy to see why this is the case. Unlike a competent adult, a child generally lacks the experience, maturity of judgment, and understanding to assess properly the things that go on around it and, in particular, to anticipate the difficulties which might arise. Consequently, he is more vulnerable to his physical and social environment than is a competent adult. For these reasons, it is of tremendous importance that the child comes to believe that, in addition to providing for him, his parents would not knowingly put him in harm's way and, moreover, that he can always retreat to their arms of protection in the face of difficulty. Needless to say, this belief could not have a more secure foundation than that the child has the conviction that his parents love him, since love, unlike praise, does not revolve around a person's performances. Of course, I do not deny that parental praise plays an important role in the child's life; it clearly serves to shape the aims and aspirations of the child. However, because parental praise is tied to the child's performances, it cannot serve to allay, if not preclude entirely, the child's fear of parental rejection, and so its fear of loss of parental support and protection.[8] This only parental love can do. For, as I have observed, love is unconditional.

Life offers no assurances against misfortune, no matter how cautious and prudent we might be. Thus, no adult could fail to be comforted by the belief that in time of need, there are those to whom he could turn for assistance, whatever they should think of his behavior. And if this holds for the competent adult, then, *a fortiori*, it holds for the inexperienced child. It is worth noting, parenthetically, that a somewhat surprising consequence of these considerations is that it is perhaps a good thing that the child does not always measure up to his parents' expectations. For it is possible for parents to disapprove of their child's behavior and yet manifest their love for him. Neither child nor parents could want for a surer sign of parental love than this.

Now, the relevant insight to be gained from the preceding discussion is that a child's feeling of basic psychological security is secured by parental approval not being the only basis for his receiving parental support and protection. More precisely, it is secured by his having the conviction that to some extent he is free to act without fear of the loss of parental support and protection on account of his behavior not meeting parental approval. And this is how it must be if the child is not to feel that his parents regard him as merely an extension of their will. Needless to say, these remarks are compatible with the fact that the child's desire to receive parental approval and to avoid parental disapproval plays a significant role in the child's being motivated to behave as his parents desire. But, it is one thing to say that such matters play a significant role in the child's life; it is quite another to say that only they do, with the implication being that parental love does not. And it is the latter, not the former, which I deny.

III

Now, clearly, approval and disapproval play an important role in the lives of adults.[9] Professional success, for instance, is very much a function of the recognition which we receive from a jury of our peers. And in a more social context, there is the inescapable fact that we value the approval of our friends. Indeed, the realization that no one group of friends is apt to be accepting of everything we do is surely part of the explanation for why we often have different circles of friends. What is particularly relevant to the concerns of this essay, however, is that not only do we want there to be strong social disapproval of behavior which is contrary to what I referred to earlier (§1) as the minimum content of law, but that fear of such disapproval is undoubtedly no small part of the explanation for why many people are minimally good citizens.[10] In view of these considerations, one might be tempted to conclude that it is not possible for the social institutions of society to be conducive to the members of society having basic psychological security, that is, psychological security which is in no way tied to approval of their social behavior. As I hope to show in what follows, this temptation should be resisted. What is more, when the importance which basic psychological security plays in the life of the child is viewed in conjunction with (i) Rousseau's observation that the love of humanity as such is impossible and (ii) the quite plausible assumption that basic psychological security continues to be important throughout our lives,[11] then it actually becomes expedient that society's social institutions are conducive to our basic psychological security.

It will be recalled that in the introduction I claimed that social institutions which are conducive to persons having self-respect are the social analogue to parental love. My reason for claiming this is not that I take social approval and disapproval of the members of society to be perfectly analogous to parental approval and disapproval of the child. Nor is it that I take this to be so of legal punishment for criminal behavior and the withdrawal of parental love. Rather, it has to do with the fact that, conceptually, social disapproval no more constitutes a legal punishment than does parental disapproval constitute a withdrawal of parental love. *And just as parents do what is certainly wrong, from the standpoint of what proper child care calls for, in regarding the withdrawal of parental love as simply a means of expressing parental disapproval, society does what is certainly wrong when it*

allows the grounds for designating behavior or lifestyles, which are in keep-
ing with the minimum content of law, as criminal to be nothing more than
that they do not meet with social approval.[12] We have a moral wrong here
because the social institutions of any society such as this are unjustly and
unfairly arranged, justice and fairness being two very significant aspects of
morality. These remarks, which I shall elaborate upon below, give us a handle on what is morally objectionable about Strict PAL.

Few things, if any, are more inimical to our conception of ourselves as beings with full moral status, and so to our having self-respect, than our being
the continuous objects of arbitrary and capricious treatment, since on no
plausible account of the moral point of view do these things count among its
defining characteristics. Now, facts about our behavior are irrelevant to our
having full moral status; this we have simply in virtue of being persons. To
be sure, a thing's behavior may be relevant in settling the epistemological
question of whether or not it is a person. (The class of persons is assumed to
not be coextensive with the class of *homo sapiens.*[13]) But, once the
epistemological question is settled in favor of a thing's being a person, then
the question of its having full moral status is settled affirmatively. What
may appear to be too strong a claim is borne out by the observation that the
grounds for why we morally ought to treat criminals fairly and justly cannot
plausibly be made to turn upon their behavior being of the appropriate sort.
Again, the argument that slavery is morally wrong is not contingent upon
whether or not those enslaved have a good moral character.[14] The institution of slavery is simply unjust and unfair.

Just and fair treatment precludes the arbitrary and capricious treatment
of persons. And as should be apparent from the preceding remarks, what I
take to be morally objectionable about Strict PAL is that its social institutions are unjustly and unfairly arranged. At least its legal institutions are.
But, then, a society's legal institutions (of which, of course, the criminal law
is a key element) are among its most important social institutions in that
they define the rights, freedoms, and privileges of the members of society;
and they provide a basis for legitimate expectations in terms of both support
from, as well as non-interference on the part of, others. The legal institutions of Strict PAL are unjustly and unfairly arranged precisely because the
only grounds upon which the pursuit of this or that lifestyle is designated as
criminal is that it does not meet with social approval. Hence, that a given
lifestyle does not meet with such approval constitutes a sufficient legal
justification for officially and publicly subjecting a person to undesirable
modes of treatment. When this is the only grounds for punishment, then
such treatment reduces to that which is arbitrary and capricious. For

punishment thus grounded is not anchored in a moral conception of how persons should be treated.

To put the point another way, whenever society's social institutions, its legal ones in particular, are arranged so that there is no conceptual space between social disapproval and grounds for punishment and, furthermore, the former is sufficient to yield the latter, then we have a case where punishment reduces to arbitrary and capricious treatment. For, nothing at all follows about the rightness or wrongness of a given instance of behavior, nothing at all follows about its reasonableness or unreasonableness, given just the fact that someone disapproves of it. Hence, in a society such as Strict PAL almost any reason can be a good reason for punishing someone, and so almost no reason at all is needed to punish someone. Obviously enough, a practice of punishment cannot be more capricious or arbitrary than this. Nor is more required in order for it to be unjust and unfair.

Now, I have claimed that persons have full moral status in virtue of the fact that they are persons. The social institutions of society are conducive to persons having this belief if and only if they are conducive to persons believing that, in virtue of their personhood, they should not be treated in an arbitrary and capricious manner. And in order to do this, social institutions must be conducive to persons having the belief that, in virtue of their personhood, significant restraints on how they can be treated follow. I maintain that any society of which these things are true engenders basic psychological security on the part of its members. For no reference is made to approval of performances; and it will be remembered that as I understand it, basic psychological security refers to that measure of psychological security which is in no way tied to approval, on the part of others, of our performances.

The above considerations should make it clear that the social institutions of Strict PAL cannot be conducive to its members having basic psychological security. The fact that there is unanimity of opinion in Strict PAL might incline one to think otherwise, since there is indeed security in numbers. Security in numbers is not, however, to be confused with basic psychological security. The former is not necessarily security which is underwritten by the social institutions of society, as the case of Strict PAL shows. For there is nothing in Strict PAL to prevent the tide of approval from flowing in an entirely different direction thus rendering as criminal behavior that which hitherto had been allowed to flourish. Should this happen, a person who found herself unmoved by the social current would be without a rock of refuge. She would find herself standing as a criminal just because people no longer approved of her life style. Needless to say, it is compatible with everything I have said that a person such as this might nonetheless have basic psychological security. For, my claim throughout this essay has been that just and fair institutions are conducive to persons having basic psychological security. I have not claimed, nor have I meant to, that a person can have basic psychological security only if the institutions of society are just and fair.

Now, since having self-respect is defined as having the belief that one has full moral status, it follows, given what has already been said, that the social institutions of society are conducive to persons having self-respect if and only if they are conducive to persons having basic psychological security. As we have just seen, the latter does not hold for Strict PAL, hence we know that the former does not as well. The fact that basic psychological security and self-respect dovetail in this way allows us to attach normative weight to the fact that the social institutions of Strict PAL are not conducive to persons having basic psychological security. For our basic psychological security as adults is tied to our having the belief that others should treat us as beings with full moral status. No one has a moral claim to our love or friendship, the case of children aside. Everyone has a moral claim to our treating them as beings with full moral status. And the social institutions of society should be conducive to everyone having the belief that this is so. (This, of course, does not mean that everyone will have it; for it does not follow from the fact that it is rational for a peron to believe something that he will.) Social institutions which are not, are unfairly and unjustly arranged.

No doubt few who have reflected upon the matter have failed to come to the conclusion that there is a connection between a just and fair society and one which is conducive to its members having basic psychological security. What may be surprising, though, is that in order to bring out the importance of this connection, we have not had to consider a society which is manifestly oppressive in the usual ways. Few would deny that the nefariousness of American slavery or Nazi Germany was not conducive to blacks and Jews, respectively, having self-respect, and so basic psychological security. But Strict PAL cannot, as I have already observed, be characterized as wicked in these ways, as its counterpart, PAL, serves to remind us. For Strict PAL, it will be remembered, just is PAL with its shared values enshrined in law (it being understood that, as I have said before, that the values in question are over and above those dictated by the minimum content of law). The difference between PAL and Strict PAL show that in order for a society to be substantially unjust and unfair, no identifiable group of persons in society need be targeted or oppressed. It shows the ease with which a society can pass from being just and fair to being neither by passing legislation, with the intention of strengthening the social fabric of society, which requires conformity to the shared values of society. For legislation which makes social approval alone the ground for designating behavior as criminal adjusts social institutions so that they no longer foster self-respect and, hence, basic psychological security among the members of society.

If Strict PAL is an unjust society for the reasons which I have advanced in this essay, then what unquestionably follows is that a morally superior society would be one where the grounds for punishment are anchored in a moral conception of how persons should be treated. At worst, such a society would be one like PAL. At best, such a society would be one in which diversity flourished. One may take this last consideration to show that maximal liberalism is morally superior to minimal liberalism, from which one then supposes it to follow that society is morally required to encourage diversity of lifestyles.[15] But this is too swift. Something can be morally superior without being morally required. The saint is morally superior to the typical moral person; yet, it would be a mistake to think that we are morally required to be saints.[16] In any case, I am content to have shown that minimal liberalism or social libertarianism is morally preferably to conservativism because conservativism of the form exhibited by Strict PAL is unfair and unjust. Moreover, we have seen that the explanation for why this is so dovetails with what I take to be a deep fact regarding our psychological nature, namely the need for basic psychological security, that is, psychological security which is not tied to approval of our behavior.

Against all of this, one may object that conservatives of the moral majority type are not as I have presented them, since they do take their moral views about how the social institutions of society should be arranged to have a moral foundation. Although this is quite true, I need only observe that reasonable and reflective people can and do differ with them on both matters of Christian theology and its implications for how society's social institutions should be arranged. Members of the moral majority, however, are unwilling to attach any importance to this fact; in particular, they attach little weight to the fact that they are imposing their conception of the good life on others. Now, if Strict PAL is morally objectionable, notwithstanding the absence of impositions of this sort, then surely it must be morally objectionable for any group to be indifferent to the fact that they are imposing their conception of the good life upon reasonable and reflective people.

Let me tempt you with an all too brief argument which might serve to buttress these last remarks. Let M-PAL stand for a society which is exactly

like PAL; but assume, now, that everyone subscribes to the correct set of
moral values and that this is known by everyone. And let SM-PAL be to
M-PAL what Strict PAL is to PAL. Anyone who maintains that there is
nothing morally objectionable about the move from M-PAL to SM-PAL
would have to hold there is nothing morally objectionable about a legal
sanction being attached to any and every moral wrong. The case for this latter proposition has not yet been made; nor do I think that it can be. Thus,
suppose it is true that any woman who intends to come to term with the
fetus she is carrying does what is morally wrong if she drinks and smokes
excessively, since these activities clearly have a deleterious affect upon the
fetus and in refraining from doing these things a woman does not sacrifice
some important good. From the truth of this supposition what does not
seem to follow — and certainly not just like that — is that it would be morally
permissible to punish legally any woman who engages in these activities.
Again, if we hold that it is morally wrong for persons to break their promises, barring reasons of a certain sort, what does not seem to follow obviously from this is that it would be morally permissible to punish legally all
persons who broke their promises without the appropriate reasons obtaining. If a society like M-PAL should ever become a reality, these considerations suggest that it is very far from being a foregone conclusion that there
would be nothing morally objectionable about the move to SM-PAL. The
case against the moral majority or sophisticated conservatives of whatever
stripe may be stronger than many have been inclined to suppose.[17]

If the arguments of this essay are sound, then we have seen that forced
uniformity of values in society, beyond those values which are in keeping
with the minimum content of law, can be very much an anthama, albeit one
that may easily masquerade as a blessing.

University of North Carolina-Chapel Hill

NOTES

* A version of this paper was presented under the title "Rights, Liberties, and Our
Psychological Nature" as part of the Public Program held in conjunction with the 10th In-
terAmerican Congress of Philosophy, 18-23 October 1981. And a version was read under the
present title at McMaster University (Canada). In addition to my colleagues, Stephen Darwall
and Gerald J. Postema, a number of other people have been kind enough to offer comments:
Bernard Boxill, Merrill Hintikka, Edmond Pincoffs, Rolf Sartorious, and Rogers Smith.

The seeds for this essay began to germinate during the Summer of 1980 during which time I was fellow at the Reason Foundation. However, my greatest debt is to the members of my NEH Interprofessions Seminar, "Competing Rights Claims in a Complex Society." It is to them that the ideas in this essay were first presented. The participants proved to be a most gracious and instructive sounding board.

This essay is an argument against the sort of legal moralism defended by, e.g., Lord Patrick Devlin, *The Enforcement of Morals* (Oxford: Oxford University Press, 1965). For a very different argument against legal moralism, see Joel Feinberg, "Legal Moralism and Freefloating Evils," *Pacific Philosophical Quarterly* 61 (1980): 122-55. Indeed, our approaches are so radically different that no attempt is made to compare the views presented here with those presented by Feinberg.

1. While liberals and libertarians generally part company on economic matters, they are generally in agreement with one another when it comes to the view that people should be free to pursue their own conception of the good life. They generally agree on the social freedoms that people should have. Hence, my use of the term social libertarianism.

2. *On Liberty*, especially ch. 3. Some of what I shall say is, I think, suggested by the writings of John Rawls, *A Theory of Justice* (Cambridge, MA: Harvcard University press, 1971), see Part III especially.

3. For an account of how I understand the concept of self-respect, see my "Morality and Our Self-Concept," *The Journal of Value Inquiry* 12 (1978): 68-78; "Rawlsian Self-Respect and the Black Consciousness Movement," *The Philosophical Forum* 9 (1979): 67-79. The expression 'full moral status' is my own. My use of it, however, is very similar, if not identical, to L. W. Sumner's use of the expression "full moral standing." See his *Abortion and Moral Theory* (Princeton, NJ: Princeton University Press, 1981), pp. 26-33.

4. In *The Concept of Law* (Oxford: Oxford University Press, 1961), ch. 9. As Postema and Smith have reminded me, the minimum content of law is for Hart very minimal indeed; not only that, reasonable people can differ over what that comes to. In introducing Hart's notion in the text, I mean only to give the reader a better handle on the kind of society I have in mind. I am not attempting to have it do work that it cannot do.

5. This point is forcefully developed in Lawrence Blum, *Friendship, Altruism, and Morality* (Boston, MA: Routledge and Kegan Paul, 1980).

6. My thinking here owes much to Gregory Vlastos, "Justice and Equality," in Richard Brandt (ed.), *Social Justice* (Englewood Cliffs, NJ: Prentice-Hall, Inc., 1962). See, also, R. W. White, *Ego and Reality in Psychoanalytic Theory, Psychological Issues*, monograph 11 (New York: International University Press, Inc., 1963), ch. 7 especially.

7. There is much to be read on this topic. I shall simply list a major work and two anthologies: John Bowlby, *Child Care and the Growth of Love* (Baltimore, MD: Penguin Books, 1953). He writes:

> [W]hat is believed to be essential for mental health is that an infant and young child should experience a warm, intimate, and continuous relationship with his mother (or permanent mother-substitute...) in which both find satisfaction and enjoyment (p. 13).

Bowlby's three volume work is *Attachment and Loss* (New York: Basic Books). For interesting discussions regarding child development, see, e.g., Jerome Bruner and Alison Garton (eds.), *Human Growth and Development* (New York: Oxford University Press, 1976) and Harry

McGurk (ed.), *Issues in Childhood Social Development* (London, England: Methuen and Co., 1978).

8. It is arguable, I believe, that Freud's account of child development is defective precisely because he failed to appreciate sufficiently the difference between parental love and parental praise. See his account of the development of the ego in, e.g., his *Civilization and Its Discontents*.

9. Thus, the enormous literature on self-esteem focuses primarily on adults. Morris Rosenberg's book, *Conceiving the Self* (New York: Basic Books, 1979), is a first-rate essay on the topic which discusses both adults and children.

10. See my remarks in note 4.

11. In *Political Economy*, Rousseau writes:
> It appears that the feeling of humanity evaporates and grows feeble in embracing all mankind, and that we cannot be affected by the calamities of Tartary or Japan in the same manner as we are by those of European nations. It is necessary in some degree to confine and limit our compassion in order to make it active.

For an illuminating account of the importance of basic psychological security in the adult life, and its connection with trust, see John Bowlby, "The Self-Reliant Personality: Some Conditions That Promote It," in Rom Harre (ed.), *Personality* (Totowa, NJ: Rowman and Littlefield, 1976): 3-24.

12. I believe that in fact parents do what is morally wrong in regarding the withdrawal of parental love as simply an expression of disapproval. But I cannot argue this here.

13. This point seems to have gained general acceptance in the philosophical literature. Cf. Michael Tooley, "Abortion and Infanticide," *Philosophy and Public Affairs* 2 (1973): 37-66.

14. Of course, one may argue, as American slave owners surely did, that a creature's inability to have a certain kind of moral character constitutes evidence that it is not a full-fledged person. But here the argument is not simply that the creature lacks the kind of moral character in question, but that it is constitutionally unable to have such a character. And it is on account of this latter point that the creature is presumed to be less than a full-fledged person. Aristotle, e.g., reasoned in this way. He held that slaves are without deliberative faculty and, therefore, have less virtue than their masters and other free men. See Aristotle's *Politics* Bk 1, ch. 13 (1260a-1260b5).

15. A not implausible reading of Dworkin is that he endorses what I call maximal liberalism. At any rate, he seems to call for something more than what I have called minimal liberalism. See his "Liberalism," in Stuart Hampshire (ed.), *Public and Private Morality* (New York: Cambridge University Press, 1978).

16. A point which J. O. Urmson masterfully develops in "Saints and Heroes," in A. I. Meldon (ed.), *Essays in Moral Philosophy* (Seattle, WA: University of Washington Press, 1958): 198-215.

17. The considerations advanced in this paragraph were prompted by some remarks from the floor by James Fishkin at the Bowling Green State University Conference on Social Justice.

THE SOCIAL THEORY OF RIGHTS

Ferdinand Schoeman

Recent analyses of moral rights have found the significance of rights to lie in the promotion of several goals: respect for persons as ends in themselves; protection of individual discretion; promotion of individual interests and protection from avoidable serious harms. Since these aspects of the significance of rights bring individuals into sharp relief against the background of social aims and practices, we might broadly regard these aspects as individualistic or atomistic.

There is a view of rights, however, which places greater emphasis on persons as social beings than does this contemporary account. While it can be shown that a more socially oriented theory of rights has actually dominated the natural rights tradition, the objective of this paper is to provide a clarification of the philosophical differences that lie between the individualistic or atomistic and the social interpretation of rights. What I shall argue is that a social theory of rights places greater emphasis on the bonds that tie persons together than does the alternative account. As a consequence of this shift in emphasis the social theory integrates more moral parameters within itself, and gives occasion for less moral conflicts than does the current analysis of rights.

In the final part of this paper I shall try to show that John Locke subscribed to the social view of rights and that accordingly his understanding of rights encompassed their function as a means to maintain equity and sociability in society.

I

According to the social theory of rights the point of rights is to help to assure that people are in a position to be participants in some society on an equitable basis. Within this view individuals are still to be understood as entitled to dignity and discretion — the features of rights which make up much of the individualistic version of rights. Also, rights are still thought to pertain to individuals. But there is more. Individuals are also to be understood to require social intercourse, not just for the satisfaction of basic vital needs but for completion of character as rational and social beings. Conceptually, rights are supposed to reflect those features of entities deserving of special moral recognition. The point of the social theory of rights is to acknowledge social character and dependence as integral features of human beings.

On this view each person is naturally a member of a universal moral community replete with duties and entitlements which together constitute the minimal bases for general human relationships. The interests human beings have in being both social and rational are so central that they constitute the bases of duties if anything at all does.

But what is meant by saying that people should be assured the role of equitable participant? To say that a person is a *participant* in society is to say that people are to be viewed as multi-facetedly connected with others, and that all interactions between persons are to be judged through that broader perspective. Requirements of continued social interdependence are to be maintained in all socially recognized relationships, including recognition of contractual agreements.

To say that the participation should be on an *equitable* basis is to say that the terms of human interdependence ought to be compatible with the realization of aspects of human nature focused upon in the individualistic interpretation of rights, viz., dignity and discretion. The reason that equity is connected here with dignity and discretion is practical. While individuals under some circumstances might bargain away their autonomy in order to obtain certain benefits, the conditions under which they are *likely* to do so are so often ones of coercion or necessity that protection from *such* inequitable bargaining positions is thought mandatory. And even when such a bargain does respect the parties to the bargain, it may still have socially degrading consequences for their progeny.

There are several important respects in which this social theory of rights differs from the orthodox, individualistic account. (1) The view of human nature is different in the individualistic and social accounts of rights. In the individualistic account social transactions are the means by which individuals attain their preestablished largely atomistic aims. Rights here represent limits or the moral boundaries of persons beyond which no one may go in an effort to achieve his aims. Within the social account of rights, essential and natural aspects of human interest include sociability and community participation. So besides focusing on moral boundaries that separate people, within this view there is a concentration on the connections between people prerequisite for community. Since individuals have an intrinsic interest in the maintenance of their community, they naturally want to structure roles and practices in such a way as to promote sociability and broadly based relationships between people. Characteristically, theories of rights focus attention on those aspects of human nature thought to be morally distinctive. What is seen as distinctive in the social theory are human social qualities. Consequently, the theory of rights reflects recognition of this social condition within which this human character can flourish. A greater sense of social responsibility is to be found within the theory of rights of the social theorists than of the individualist theorist. Such a community orientation does not necessarily mean expropriation of the individual for the benefit of society or the dilution of each individual's interests in discretion and dignity.

(2) A second major difference between the way rights are conceived in the individualistic and social traditions concerns the way rights are related to other moral values. On the individualistic view of rights, what rights we have frequently come into conflict with other moral values. Given the importance of rights generally, there are high threshold conditions set before it would be legitimate to withhold enforcement of the right. But what is important here is that these other values are typically seen as external to rights, requiring that we merely balance recognition of rights — somehow fixed — on the one hand with recognition of potentially competing values on the other. Consideration A is *external* to consideration B if reflection on A is not morally germane to the issue of how B is to be interpreted, even though it may be germane to determining whether B morally dominates in a particular situation.

Within the individualistic theory, the values that are taken to be determinative of rights, and hence internal to the existence and interpretation of rights, are individualistic goods: individual dignity, individual freedom or discretion, individual interests whether fixed by nature or by nature and society. Philosophers who represent the ground of rights as completely individualistic include: H. L. A. Hart (whose focus is on the centrality of freedom),[1] John Rawls (whose focus is on the means by which rational individuals assure themselves the opportunity to pursue their own conception of the good),[2] Joel Feinberg (whose focus is on the dignity of the individual and on the goal of providing for the satisfaction of basic needs and for the promotion of individual interests),[3] Ronald Dworkin (whose focus is, depending on the level of analysis, either on the provision of equal respect for persons or on the maximization of satisfactions of strictly personal preferences)[4] and Tim Scanlon (whose focus is on provision of biologically and socially determined needs and individual discretion).[5] Of course, in saying that these theorists are individualistic or atomistic in their theory of rights I am not claiming that their general *moral* theory is of the atomistic sort — for this is not true in the case of any of the theorists mentioned. It is only to say that what their theories of rights emphasize is this atomistic character of persons.

What is remarkable about this treatment of rights is the absence of an effort to connect explicitly requirements of social well-being with the determination of whether there are rights to various things in the first place. As Bruce Ackerman has pointed out, it is part of the ordinary person's understanding of a right that it does not entitle a person to acts "unduly harmful to others."[6] This is not just meant to say that one person's rights end where another's begin, for precisely what is at issue is how to figure out where rights begin and end.

Within the social theory, values external to rights on the individualistic theory become internal. What is meant by saying that such values are *internal* is that in the very process of judging whether there is a general or specific right, account is taken of a whole range of values including not just needs of specifiable individuals but also the actual or projected effects on social intercourse and on a wide range of interpersonal relationships.

One might ask at this point whether, within the social theory of rights, concern for social relations generally functions as a constraint on the legitimate exercise of rights or whether such concern goes into the very determination of what rights there are in the first place. By saying that social values are internalized I mean to indicate that entitlements which would have generally deleterious effects on social relationships from a broad range of perspectives would be disqualified from the start. It is not that we have the standard picture of rights balanced by utilitarian concerns, where the latter, but not the former are socially cognizant. It is that rights too reflect social awareness. Even so, there will still be occasions when rights conflict in particular situations with other morally recognizable desiderata. But since many of the practices which have a tendency to socially disenfranchise individuals are disqualified from being considered entitlements at the start, there is less conflict between rights and these other dimensions than there is in the case of the individualistic theory of rights.

An illustration of a situation over which the social and individualistic theories of rights might differ could prove helpful at this point. Richard Titmus has argued that the commercialization of blood for use in transfusions represents an assault on some of our very basic ideas of common bondage. The sale of body organs has been similarly cited as an improper object of commercial exchange. So too with children, even at the infant stage. The concern in each of these cases is not that the parties to the exchange are made worse off as a result. Persons who want blood, healthy vital organs, or children might often welcome the opportunity. So might the potential sellers. The problem is the undesirable shift in the context of human relationships that commercialization of these items might bring in its wake.

Someone concerned with such consequences might plausibly argue that no one has a right to sell his child, his blood, his kidney even though the object is his (in some sense). His reason for denying that there is a right to such transactions is his concern for the consequences of allowing such a practice — consequences which he believes includes socially demoralizing changes in attitudes.

II

A question which must be addressed at this point is whether notions like 'social value' or 'sociability' don't ultimately come down to the same things as the promotion of the dignity, interests, and needs of individuals.

In arguing that there is a morally pressing alternative to the individualistic theory of rights one does not have to be making a metaphysically ambitious claim that there are goods which do not ultimately redound to the benefit of individuals. It is enough to say that there are goods for the individual which derive exclusively from relationships with others and to note that some such relationships appear to be central to the human way of being. This is easiest to see in the case of the parent/child relationship, the husband/wife relationship, and friendships. For the advocate of the social theory of rights, there is also a good of community, which has associated with it a broad conception of responsibility to others.

The way in which the good to individuals of certain kinds of relationships operate may not be best thought of as an instrumentality. It may be rather that because of the nature of the creature it flourishes in certain kinds of environments and languishes in others. The ways in which persons flourish in relationships with others simply may not be possible outside of a supportive, social context, independent of what else is provided. It may even be that many of the goods we regard as basic and seek after would have no meaning to us outside of our relationships to others. Aristotle remarks that without friends, no one would choose to live even if he had all other goods.[7] One might even argue the thesis that equality, in some sense, is important because of the impact a situation of gross disparity has on the capacity of those worst off to maintan their standing as social and moral beings.

When Richard Titmus summarizes what he finds morally objectionable about the commercialization of blood 'donation' systems, while he is concerned with the effects on the sense of responsibility for, and connection with, others, he speaks in terms that have an obvious impact on individual welfare.

From our study of the private market in blood in the United States we have concluded that the commercialization of blood and donor relationships represses the expression of altruism, erodes the sense of community, lowers scientific standards, limits both personal and professional freedoms, sanctions the making of profits in hospitals and clinical laboratories, legalizes hostility between doctor and patients, subjects critical areas of medicine to the laws of the marketplace, places immense social costs on those least able to bear them — the poor, and the inept — increases the danger of unethical behavior in various sectors of medical science and practice, and results in situations in which proportionally more and more blood is supplied by the poor, the unskilled...[8]

On a metaphysically more ambitious scale, there have been some recent attempts to think of rights as promoting goals which may not be reducible to individual interests in dignity, discretion, or satisfaction of basic biological and social needs. In his essay called "Rights, Goals, and Fairness," Tim Scanlon has proposed fairness and equality as rights-directed goals which in principle may be valued out of proportion to the extent to which they promote individual interests. (p. 85) This partial diremption of rights from individual interests opens up the possibility that a social policy of enforced rights may violate the Pareto efficiency standard since justice may order social state A over social state B even though all the individuals involved may prefer B to A. Amartya Sen, in his essay "Liberty, Unanimity and Rights," also questions the compatibility of enforcement of rights and Pareto efficiency.[9]

What is noteworthy here is that a goal like equality is a value that applies to a system of distribution, is essentially an interpersonal objective, and can vary, in principle, independently of the individual well-being of all the individuals within its scope of application. The goals of equity and sociability are to be similarly conceived. While in general they promote the interests of the individuals concerned, they are essentially social concepts and have potential moral gravity even if at odds with the individual interests of all concerned.

There are both moral and metaphysical differences between the individualistic and the social theories of rights. Not only do they describe human nature differently, they entitle people to different things and even conceive differently the issue of how entitlements are to be settled. As already mentioned, within the social theory of rights which rights persons actually possess are determined in part by conditions of sociability and social welfare. Since these two conditions may change dramatically over time, it is somewhat easier to conceive on this view than it is on the individualistic view how it is that rights have an historical dimension. There are certain limitations on bargining which those who defend the individualistic view of rights have difficulty dealing with but which have a natural account within the social view. Such limitations have to do mainly with bargains in which one of the parties is in a condition of duress or necessity. Welfare rights too come to fit more naturally in the social account than in the individualistic account of rights.

Philosophers have debated the issue of why rights or theories of rights are specifically important. Typically this debate has been carried out at the level of asking whether various interpersonal relationships which are morally affected by the existence of relevant rights can be suitably redescribed using the language of duties and obligation. Though what philosophers have to say about this issue is enlightening, there is something else at issue. To bring this out we shall begin with the reducibility issue.

At the core of natural rights theories is a concern with individual freedom and discretion. While some of the limitations on people which arise as a result of this distribution of limited sovereignty can conceivably be elaborated in terms of duties, the moral significance of such duties might not be so evident from a theory restricted to talk of duties and obligations.

There are rights we attribute to people merely on the basis of regarding others as having a certain duty or obligation. For instance, since we think that the phone company has a duty to list information about customers accurately we might say that customers have a right to such accuracy. *Such* rights are adequately described in terms of correlative duties without loss. There are other rights we attribute to persons, however, where the refinements of analysis in terms of specific duties would be inherently incomplete. The right to have a say in one's government or the right to an education would be examples. The reason is that typically talk of rights has a broader purpose.

A theory of rights at its broader level serves to describe a moral picture of what it is to be a person. While this picture has some well defined rules to it, it also has an indeterminate import in that it provides for novel ways of drawing analogies, of making connections, and of morally describing a situation. Such pictures, for all their vagueness, systematize or unify particular moral duties and particular moral sensitivities as well as give direction to efforts aimed at understanding and interpreting these duties and sensitivities. Rights represent efforts at making sense of our moral world as well as efforts at making the world something that reflects a moral sense. Consequently rights play an organizational role and an evolutionary role that lists of duties cannot accomplish.

Rights, as entitlements to discretion, provide people with the opportunity to participate in, or identify with, the particular kind of social order they deem desirable, since rights frequently leave to individual judgment the problem of resolving conflicts of interest. Rather than merely representing a moral rationale for the rational pusuit of self-interest unencumbered by a concern for the consequences of one's pursuit on others, the social conception of rights presupposes a public understanding of a kind of social order which informs and limits individual strivings.

III

While there is nothing novel about expressions of dissatisfaction with the individualistic view of rights or with the recounting of theories of rights which emphasized the social rather than the individualistic character of rights, interpreting John Locke as a central figure in this social theory of rights camp should be of some contemporary interest since Locke is widely regarded as the archetypical individualistic interpreter of rights.[10] C. B. Macpherson in his book *The Political Theory of Possessive Individualism* claims, "Locke's astounding achievement was to base property rights on natural right and natural law, and then to remove all the natural law limits from the property right." (p. 198)[11] And, "Fundamentally it [Locke's individualism] consists in making the individual the natural proprietor of his own person and capacities owing nothing to society for them." (p. 225) To cite another example of such an interpretation, Gary Wills has recently argued in his book *Inventing America* that the Declaration of Independence must have been primarily inspired by the Scottish moralists and not by Locke since the Declaration reflects a communitarian view of rights.[12]

To cite one final example of this standard intepretation of Locke we might look to Robert Nozick's book, *Anarchy, State and Utopia*. Nozick is explicit in interpreting Locke's theory of property as one which satisfies an 'historical principles' type of justice rather than 'end-results' principles. (p. 181)[13] A theory of justice is basically of the end-result type in case a distribution can be judged just or unjust by reflecting on the distribution structure at any one time, without reference to how the particular distribution came about or to specifically who has what. A theory of justice is basically of the historical sort in case human activity can create differences in entitlements, so that two distributions can be structurally the same but not equally just depending upon who has what. (pp. 153-55) Even the Lockean proviso that people are to retain opportunities to appropriate, Nozick says, is "not an 'end-state principle'; it focuses on a particular way that appropriative actions affect others, and not on the structure of the situation that results." (p. 181) But for Locke, whether a person is entitled to x, for some x's, is dependent in part on what others need, independent of desert. Like it or not, this is redistributionist or welfare-oriented in a way that is obscured by Nozick's labelling of Locke as historically oriented. For as Nozick usually interprets historical principles of justice, they exclude just these sort of considerations.

Theories of natural rights like Locke's are best understood as part of an overall theory aimed at stabilizing equality between people. Specifically, natural rights were not typically regarded as entitling people to unrestricted liberties even within the domain explicitly covered by rights; furthermore certain natural duties were understood as restrictions on the free exercise and appreciation of rights. Both natural rights and natural duties converge on sustaining a sort of equality between people within society. Maintaining this equality promotes one of the fundamental interests people have as moral entities. Also an interest in promoting sociability imposes a concern for equality since the social structure has to be such that generally each person profits from his association with others. (Note the extent to which this diverges from Macpherson's interpretation: "And only if men are assumed to be equally capable of shifting for themselves, can it be thought equitable to put them on their own, and leave them to confront each other in the market without the protections which the old natural law doctrine upheld." (p. 245))

While it is analytically important for the issues being discussed that I elaborate on the meaning of equality and the limits that a conception of it imposes on the class of legitimate social arrangements, a number of problems make supplying such a conception difficult. In the first place, natural law and natural rights writers rarely discussed the exact import of natural equality directly, though they were insistent that it did have consequences of note. Second, in line with the general picture of rights I want to attribute to the natural rights thinkers, the limitations imposed by a concern for equality cannot be specified *a priori*, except in a vague manner. One reason is that while equality as a principle requires that people should not fall below a certain level of bargaining power *vis à vis* other people, that level varies with social economic conditions. Another reason why requirements of equality cannot be precisely characterized is that new requirements of equality may emerge as the means for promoting social equality become more effective.

The vague *a priori* conception of equality which is operative can be characterized thus: *no person should be in a position such that to maintain his life or that of his dependents or socially determined minimal resources that he should be forced to subject himself to the complete control of another.* While much more than this is involved in explicating equality, I stress this aspect of equality because it contains three key features:

(1) recognition of restricitons imposed by the sociability criterion; (2) socially relative crieteria of adequate levels of life; and (3) an appreciation for the volatility of initially equal positions.

The most obvious points to begin with in bringing out the egalitarian and communitarian limitations that Locke places on the exercise of rights are his two restrictions on the original acquisition of property: the non-spoilage condition (II, sects. 31, 46, and 51) and the sufficiency condition (II, sects, 27, 33, and 36).[14] These conditions, however, are problematic from a number of perspectives. First of all, these limitations on proprietorship may apply only to the condition of original acquisition. More importantly, with the introduction of money the non-spoilage condition on acquisition and holdings ceases to be an effective limit. Precisely when the sufficiency condition would seem to have an independent role to play in limiting holdings, it is dropped from the discussion. (See Macpherson, p. 203-04, 208)

The non-spoilage condition on acquisition allows a person to take from the common stock whatever he wants so long as (1) no one else has already appropriated it and (2) so long as what is acquired will not spoil while in his possession. The sufficiency condition requires that when one appropriates something for himself out of the common stock, as much and as good is left for others. Prior to the introduction of money the sufficiency condition was superfluous as an effective limit on acquisition since the non-spoilage condition alone suffices to assure adequate material advantages to all who seek them. After the introduction of money, Locke rarely, if ever, mentions sufficiency as a limitation on acquisition or holdings even though it is only after the introduction of money that the sufficiency condition offers itself as an effective limit on acquisition and holdings. Thus if the sufficiency condition is to be thought to be part of Locke's overall concern with stabilizing equality after the introduction of money, evidence has to be imported from other parts of Locke's theory.

Such evidence is available and can be associated with the following political and economic principles: (1) Those in a condition of extreme need have a title to assistance from those with abundance; (2) No person may take advantage of the necessity of another and thereby benefit from another's distress; (3) Each person is under a general duty not to harm the essential interests of others and even has a duty to promote those interests when one can do so without jeopardizing himself; (4) Equity of benefits to all is a precondition of the legitimacy of all non-natural institutions, including private property and political organizations. These four principles reflect explicit and traditional stabilizing features on the original equality into which men are born and are designed to promote sociability. Locke was

aware of the fact that without restrictions on both the means of achievement of social good and on the exercise of individual rights that circumstances might provide some with the leverage to force others into a position of inferiority. While Locke is not sufficiently precise on these points,
he is nonetheless emphatic, as we shall now go on to illustrate.

(1) *The right to the means of subsistence.*

> But we know God hath not left one man so to the mercy of another that he may starve
> him if he please; God...has given no one of his children such a property in his peculiar
> portion of the things of this world, but that he has given his needy brother a right to the
> surplusage of his goods; so that cannot justly be denied him when his pressing want calls
> for it. And therefore no man could ever have a just power over the life of another, by
> right of property in land or possessions; since 'twould always be a sin in any man of
> estate, to let his brother perish for want of affording him relief out of his plenty. As
> justice gives to every man a title to the product of his honest industry, and the fair acquisi-
> tion of his ancestors descended to him, so *charity gives every man a title to so much out of
> another's plenty, as will keep him from extreme want, when he has no means to subsist
> otherwise.* (I, 42) (Emphasis added)

Locke does not elaborate on the degree of want a person must experience
before his laying claim on another's possession is legitimized, though one is
given to interpret him as reserving this right to a life or death situation. Nor
does Locke elaborate what measures the abjectly poor may take to avail
themselves of their entitlement to the means of subsistence. Nor, surprisingly, does he concern himself with the potential responsibility of the needy
person for his particular plight. Yet in characteristic medieval fashion charity is not taken to be supererogatory, but enforceably mandatory.

It is worth pointing out here a contrast glossed over in interpreting what is
taken as God's intention. Surely one of God's purposes in giving the earth to
man in common is the benefit of mankind as a whole — an advantage to the
natural community of mankind. But in this passage it is not social good
which is emphasized but individual title to be free from extreme want — a title claimed without reference to the effect on the social good. It is important
to keep these two rationales distinct: equitable distribution and promotion
of the common good. While the latter relates to reasons of state and public
necessity as judged by those in authority, a doctrine well established in
Roman law, the former is individual in its focus and is grounded in consideration of fairness.[15] The principle applicable here is that people should
benefit from, or at least not be disadvantaged maximally because of, their
participation in conventional institutions whose point is the promotion of
individual social benefit. Rational consent to the conventions presupposes
such limits on allowable consequences of the conventions. Recognizing this
limitation on the functioning of conventions for Locke and for many of his

natural law predecessors is a crucial aspect of the historical thesis being argued here. It indicates the way in which the original equality and common property maintain a regulative effect on emergent social and economic conditions.

The right to the means of subsistence is cited in the *Second Treatise* in discussing the rights of conquerors over the possessions of those conquered, for purposes of reparation.

> The fundamental law of nature being that all, as much as may be, should be preserved it follows that if there be not enough fully to satisfy both, viz. for the conqueror's losses and the children's maintenance, he that hath any to spare must remit something of his satisfaction and give way to the pressing and preferable title of those who are in danger to perish without it. (183)

As we shall go on to show such rights to assistance serve to do more than keep men alive. It is an essential part of a theory in which equality is to be preserved.

(2) *No person is to take advantage of another's necessity.*

> And therefore no man could ever have a just power over the life of another, by right of property in land or possessions.... And a man can no more make use of another's necessity, to force him to become his vassal, by withholding that relief God requires him to afford the wants of his brother than he that has more strength can seize upon the weaker, master him to his obedience, and with a dagger at his throat offer him death or slavery. (I, 42)

The points to be focused upon here for our purposes are as follows: (1) Differences in possessions are not allowed to evolve into overly great disparities in bargaining power; i.e., moral relationships must be maintained as between relative equals. (2) One man must not be liable to become the slave of another because of necessity or dire circumstances; to take advantage of a person's dependency is morally comparable to coercion. (Lest Locke be thought uniquely overly sentimental in drawing this comparison, we might note that not only was such a comparison common in the writings of natural law writers who preceded Locke, but that Adam Smith uses the same analogy in his *Wealth of Nations*, Britannica Great Books edition, p. 55.) (3) The restrictions on the types of legitimate agreements here introduced would constitute a kind of sanctimonious indifference to the plight of those in abject circumstances were it not conjoined with the right of those in situations of extreme want to charitable relief—a right previously discussed. For without such a right those with the means others require to sustain life could simply refuse to bargain, not being content with a fair price. If the person with the desired essential goods is not satisfied with a fair price he has no right to withhold these goods since others—the needy—are entitled to them, if not in return for a fair price, than at no cost at all.

Significantly, Pufendorf, one of Locke's natural law predecessors, is most explicit in limiting agreements and the effects of agreements to ranges within which people can remain on a level of relative equality. He is at pains to underscore what I have been terming stabilizing features of human intercourse. All institutions which are the result of human agreement must be understood as maintaining people in a position of relative equality. No man may rightfully acquire a position from which he could effectively force others to become his slaves because of disparity in bargaining power, even if such disparity results from wholly innocent acts:

> To all this we reply that it is, indeed, within the power of men to make by occupancy unoccupied spaces their own, but on the condition that they bear in mind that God gave the world not to one man or another, but to all mankind, and that men are at the same time equal by nature. *Therefore, that tacit pact between those who were the first to divide things, on granting to occupiers those things which did not fall under the first division, can by no means be extended to such a thing by the possession of which one man could oppress all others with a most unjust servitude, or secure the most important advantages, which would otherwise belong to them.* And this especially because such a circumstance could not have occurred to the makers of that tacit pact. *Of The Law of Nature and Nations* (IV, V, s. 9) (emphasis added)

(3) *Limited altruism, sociability and Pareto-efficiency.*

> The state of nature has a law of nature to govern it, which obliges everyone; and reason which is that law teaches all mankind who will but consult it that being all equal and independent no one ought to harm another in his life, health, liberty, or possessions.... And being furnished with like faculties, sharing all in one communing of nature, there cannot be supposed any such subordination among us that may authorize us to destroy one another, as if we were made for another's uses, as the inferior ranks of creatures are for our's. Everyone as he is bound to preserve himself and not to quit his station wilfully, so by the like reason, when his own preservation comes not in competition, ought he, as much as he can, to preserve the rest of mankind, and may not unless it be to do justice to an offender, take away or impair the life, or what tends to the preservation of the life, liberty, health, limb or goods of another. (II,6)

In addition to explicitly giving people responsibilities for the welfare of others, there is embedded in this passage a condition of Pareto-optimality (operating when circumstances are favorable), laid not just upon the state as a representative of all, but upon each actor. The principle requires that in achieving one's own ends others not be made any worse off.

Of course such a restriction requires definition since literally interpreted it may morally preclude all actions as well as all inactions just in case each of our possible courses of action or inaction has undesirable externalities from somebody's perspective. And often enough it is the case that one party's increased assets do work to the detriment of other parties competitively engaged with the former. If the principle is to be salvaged it must be interpreted in such a way as to be operative only under certain conditions, such as a condition indicating that some high threshold of serious and deleterious consequences must be reached before the principle becomes morally effective.

(4) *Deviations from the natural state and the function of consent.*

As did other natural law theorists before him, Locke considers man's prepolitical condition to be a natural community of all men, each motivated to live in accord with natural duties by natural inclination and by reflection on conditions conducive to society. Other principles we live by, while not absolutely prerequisite for community existence, are conducive to it or productive of sufficient human convenience to warrant such restrictions as they may require. For this additional set of non-natural principles to have any binding force on individual consciences, they have to be thought of as constitutive of institutions to which people have consented. For this consent to be supposed tacitly given, each participant must be thought to benefit from his adoption of the rules of the practice. All restrictions over and above those deemed essential for community existence must be supposed as part of a voluntary practice individuals engage in for reasons of their own. Thus political inequality, political obligation, the division of property, the disparity in holdings, the introduction of money and the attendant recognition of non-natural sources of value can all be recognized as legitimate only on condition that those who are affected by them find them useful for the preservation of their lives and liberties and for the promotion of the public good. (I, 131) Deviations from the natural state must not, overall, adversely affect anyone, and especially not those whose cooperation and recognition is required. Otherwise their consent is neither free nor rational.

The mere elaboration of rights does not exhaust or even sufficiently ground social philosophy for Locke. What lies at the basis of his theory is a vision of conditions which assure the equitable participation of each in a rational community. This vision requires practices besides rights, or besides the kind of rights to non-interference some of Locke's readers judge to be the whole of his position. I have tried to show that Locke introduced stabilizing features into his theory which, along with rights to non-inference, help to assure persons a kind of social and material minimum. These stabilizing features are ones which may seriously tax individual and social resources and limit otherwise free bargaining between individuals. The binding character of such stabilizing principles is not for Locke the result of a convention and is not dependent on human will at all. Provisions for stabilizing equality and life itself are part of one's prepolitical or natural duties, which limit the kinds of agreements individuals can legitimately make or be thought to consent to rationally. There is for Locke an objective higher good, a vision of an ideal social order, which must be achieved independent of individual preferences. Such is the heritage of natural law.[16]

University of South Carolina

NOTES

1. "Are There Any Natural Rights?" in *Political Philosophy*, ed. A. Quinton, (Oxford, 1967), pp. 53-66.

2. *A Theory of Justice* (Cambridge, Mass., 1971).

3. *Social Philosophy* (Englewood Cliffs, 1973), Chapters 4-6, "The Nature and Value of Rights," *Journal of Value Inquiry*, 4 (1970), pp. 243-57, "The Rights of Animals and Unborn Generations," in W. T. Blackstone, (ed.) *Philosophy and Environmental Crisis* (Athens, 1974), pp. 43-68, and "Voluntary Euthanasia and the Inalienable Right to Life," *Philosophy and Public Affairs*, 7 (1978), pp. 93-123.

4. *Taking Rights Seriously* (Cambridge, Mass., 1977).

5. "Preference and Urgency," *Journal of Philosophy* 72 (1975), pp. 655-70, and "Rights, Goals and Fairness," *Erkenntnis* 11 (1977), pp. 81-85.

6. *Private Property and the Constitution* (New Haven, 1977), pp. 97ff.

7. *Nicomachean Ethics*, 1155a5.

8. *The Gift Relationship: From Human Blood to Social Policy* (New York, 1971), pp. 245-46.

9. *Economica* 42 (1976), pp. 217-45.

10. Of course, many writers have appreciated Locke's theory of rights as based in part on social concerns. These include: John Dunn, *Political Thought of John Locke* (Cambridge, 1969); J. Tully, *A Discourse on Property* (Cambridge, 1980); Richard Tuck, *Natural Rights Theories* (Cambridge, 1980); J. Waldron, "Enough and As Good Left For Others," *Philosophical Quarterly*, 29 (1979), pp. 319-28; M. Seliger, *The Liberal Politics of John Locke* (London, 1968); K. Olivecrona, "Locke on the Origin of Property," *Journal of the History of Ideas*, 35 (1974); J. P. Day, "Locke on Property," *Philosophical Quarterly*, 16, (1966), 207-20.

11. *The Political Theory of Possessive Individualism* (Oxford, 1962).

12. *Inventing America* (Garden City, 1978).

13. *Anarchy, State and Utopia* (New York, 1974).

14. All citations to Locke are from *Two Treatises of Government* (New York, 1964).

15. See G. Post, "Ration Publicae Utilitatis, Ratio Status, and Reason of State 1100-1300," in Post, *Studies in Medieval Legal Thought* (Princeton, 1964).

16. I wish to express gratitude to Quentin Skinner, David Lyons, Jules Coleman, Joel Feinberg, Jeffrie Murphy, Patrick Hubbard, Joseph Strayer, Victor Goldberg, Michael Gardner, and Barry Loewer for helpful discussion and encouragement on this paper or on topics addressed therein.

TWO DOGMAS ABOUT TAXATION

David A. Hoekema

According to proverb, death and taxes are the two inescapable realities of human life; but philosophers have had a great deal more to say about death than about taxes. To redress the balance, I shall offer in this paper some suggestions toward a theory of justice in taxation.

That there are controversial economic and political questions concerning taxation is daily evident in the newspaper. That taxes pose important and controversial philosophical questions seems equally evident, and any thorough exploration of political justice must take up the question of fairness in taxation. I cannot provide here a comprehensive theory of justice in taxation. Instead I shall undertake the more modest task of suggesting principles which would govern a fair tax system and refuting two dogmas which are widely but uncritically accepted: that fair taxation consists in equitable distribution of the costs of government, and that the progressive income tax is the fairest tax available to us.

Two assumptions will simplify the discussion. First, my primary concern will be the present federal tax system in the United States, in which the personal income tax provides by far the greatest share of revenue; and I will assume that any alternative tax system must provide approximately the same total amount of revenue as the present system of federal taxes. Second, I will not address the issue of revenue *vs.* debt financing but will assume that government programs and services must be financed from current revenues.[1]

Taxation is the enforced collection of payments from individuals (and legal "persons" such as corporations) to government. Its primary purpose seems obvious: to provide the funds necessary for government activities. If the purpose of government, in simplest terms, is to provide necessary services and promote the common good, taxes are a necessary means to that end.

Only if taxes are compulsory can full compliance be maintained. If taxes were voluntary, many would choose not to pay and the rest would bear a disproportionate burden. Therefore, taxes must be collected by coercive means, with the use of coercive threats. Coercion consists in inducing a person to act in a certain way by threatening intolerable harm if she fails to comply.[2] Because it interferes with an individual's ability to choose her actions, coercion is presumptively wrong. But coercive measures can be justified in the case of taxation on the ground that only by the use of coercion can the burden of taxes be spread fairly among the members of society.

Since taxation is necessary to maintain and support government, Robert Nozick's claim in *Anarchy, State, and Utopia* that income taxation is equivalent to forced labor is imprecise and misleading.[3] The analogy seems designed not to shed light on the nature of taxation but rather to call up strong negative attitudes toward forced labor, attitudes which derive from its historical association with slavery and military impressment. Taxation is not at all like these forms of forced labor: the taxpayer remains free to choose what work he will do and, if he chooses, to quit working and owe no taxes.

Even if there are some similarities between forced labor and taxation of income, the parallel offers us no independent reason to object to income taxation but borrows what force it has from Nozick's argument, earlier in his book, against the modern state. Nozick believes a state ought to do no more than provide minimal protective services to its citizens. But if, contrary to his argument, it is proper for a state to provide a broad range of programs and services, then it is also proper for government to require our support in doing so. I cannot here undertake to answer Nozick's argument for a quasi-anarchist state; let it suffice to observe that every modern state is far more extensive than Nozick would permit, and yet few consider all modern states unjust on that account. If the modern state is legitimate, then so is compulsory taxation, since it is a necessary means to its ends.

It should be noted that, in my account, the legitimacy of taxation depends crucially on the legitimacy of the government imposing the tax. Compulsory taxation is justified as a means to the legitimate ends of government; but a government which is not pursuing its legitimate ends may have no right to levy taxes. A government is legitimate, let us say, if it provides necessary services to citizens, seeks the common good, and is responsive to the will of the governed: such a government can properly require our support through taxes. But a dictatorial and repressive government, one which places the good of a few above the common good and fails to respond to its subjects' will, has no right to tax, for we have no obligation to assist dictators.

Similarly, even in a reasonably just state there may be circumstances in which citizens ought not to pay taxes. If tax monies are used to support government activities that are clearly unjust, the above justification for compulsory taxation is inappropriate. If, for example, a government is using tax revenues to wage a war which is clearly unjust or which is supported by entrenched financial interests against the public will, a strong case can be made for refusal to pay taxes — stronger, I think, than a case based solely on personal moral objection to war. We may sometimes have an obligation to support activities we dislike or disapprove, but we have no obligation to support injustice.

But fair taxation requires not only that the taxing government be legitimate but also that taxes be imposed in a fair and equitable manner. And this is my primary concern here: what constitutes fair taxation?

Economists have analyzed fairness as consisting of two elements: "horizontal equity," or equal taxation of persons equally situated, and "vertical equity," or fair apportionment of the tax burden among those differently situated.[4] Both are difficult to define. Horizontal equity seems a simple enough principle; but should *persons* or *households* equally situated pay the same tax? And what standard should determine one's economic situation — income, wealth, property, or something else?[5]

These questions are linked to questions about vertical equity, for the standard which measures comparative economic position will also identify those equally situated. Vertical equity is often defined as taxation according to "taxable capacity" or "ability to pay."[6] It seems reasonable to ask that each person should make an approximately equal sacrifice in support of government activities. And if we assume that the income needed to satisfy basic needs is the same for everyone, it follows that those with large incomes have more money to spend as they wish than those with small incomes. It is only fair to require those who are able to pay more in taxes to do so.

The notion of progressive or graduated taxation has become widely accepted in a remarkably brief period. Little more than a century ago a British author fumed that "the very name, graduation, stinks in the nostrils of wealthy men" because it represents "a filching from rich men a payment for that which they do not receive."[7] Even John Stuart Mill opposed progressive taxation.[8] Today, whatever its lingering odor in the nostrils of the wealthy, graduated taxation is seldom seriously opposed, even though the rate of graduation is still a subject of heated debate.

Three different measures of ability to pay have been suggested in the economic literature: equal absolute sacrifice, equal proportional sacrifice, and equal marginal sacrifice.[9] All three have serious defects. In the first place, none is operational: we do not know how to translate dollars into utility levels.[10] Second, all three standards assume that the optimum distribution of taxes can be determined by summation of individual gains and losses. They assume, in other words, that there is no social welfare function distinct from the aggregate of individual utility functions.

More important than these specific problems is the fundamental assumption which underlies the explanation of fairness in terms of taxable capacity: the dogma that fair taxation consists in equitable distribution of the costs of government. This assumption seriously oversimplifies the notion of fair taxation, of which equitable spreading of the tax burden, whether measured by absolute, proportional, or marginal sacrifice, is only one element.

A second criterion of fairness in taxation, I propose, is that taxes ought to *limit inequalities of wealth and income*. Progressive taxes are fair, and necessary in a just society, not simply because they impose an equal sacrifice but also because they help to control accumulations of wealth and inequalities of income.

I am not arguing that taxation should *eliminate* inequality but am making the more modest claim that a just society must *limit* inequalities when they exceed a certain degree. This claim might be supported in several ways. Some will argue that economic inequality is inherently unjust. Others, including Rawls, hold that inequality can be justified only if it benefits the least well-off.[11] From a more pragmatic standpoint, it might be argued that great inequality breeds envy and resentment, encourages the poor to turn to crime, and stirs up political unrest.[12]

But the most important reason why taxes must limit inequality is more closely connected with our notion of a legitimate government, which requires responsiveness to the will of citizens. It is because wealth creates political power, above all, that it must be subjected to limits. In a democracy, the wealthy can translate their economic power into political power in many ways, such as campaign contributions, ideological advertising, and influence on associates. They can shape laws and policies legally, through lobbying, and illegally, through bribery (and the differences between them may be subtle). Inequality of wealth, therefore, can nullify the political equality which is essential in a democracy, and it can thus undermine the citizens' power to direct the actions of their government.

The subversion of democratic processes can also be controlled directly, through laws governing political activities, and I do not mean to deny that such laws are appropriate and can be reasonably effective. I am claiming only that economic inequality, if it is subject to no limits, must at some point threaten political equality; and that claim, I think, few would dispute.

Fairness in taxation, I have argued, includes at least two elements: equitable distribution of the costs of government and limitation of inequalities. In practical terms, these two standards require graduated tax rates, at least in the higher brackets. That the rich are able to pay more taxes is not the only reason for requiring them to do so. Rather, they ought to pay higher tax rates because we all have a duty to cooperate in a system which limits economic inequality in order to preserve political equality.

What kind of taxes would satisfy these standards? I cannot develop my proposals here in detail, but I will sketch briefly the serious shortcomings of the present federal tax system and will suggest an alternative set of taxes.

Taxes may be attached to any of three economic phenomena: income, wealth, or consumption.[13] And each of these may serve as the basis for either a direct personal tax or an indirect or *ad rem* tax on things or transactions.[14]

These three bases and two kinds of tax provide six categories of tax, each of which has been employed at one time or another by modern industrial societies. Sales and excise taxes are *ad rem* taxes on consumption; the property tax is an *ad rem* tax on a specific category of wealth. The federal government levies both a personal income tax and an *ad rem* tax on income in the form of Social Security taxes. Net wealth taxes are unfamiliar in the United States but familiar in Europe; they have been in force in many European countries, including all of the Scandinavian countries, for most of this century.[15] A direct personal tax on consumption was proposed by Mill and later by British economist Nicholas Kaldor,[16] but it has been put into practice, briefly, only in India and Sri Lanka.[17]

Of these six types, the United States now places by far the greatest reliance on the personal income tax, which provided 47% of total federal revenues in 1980, for example.[18] Is the income tax a fair tax, according to the standards cited above? It appears reasonably fair: the level of compliance is high, and tax rates are graduated, under the recently revised schedule, from zero to 50%.

But study of actual tax payments suggest that the appearance of fairness is deceptive. In 1978, for example, when the maximum nominal rate of tax was 77%, taxpayers with incomes greater than $1 million paid an average of less than 50% of their taxable income in federal income tax.[19] And when undeclared and nontaxable income is included, the rate of tax is far lower: one study found that taxpayers with more than $1 million annual income actually paid only 14.5% of their income in taxes.[20]

Even when we look only at declared and taxable income, the actual rate of income tax is only mildly progressive with increasing income.[21] When we add state and local taxes to the federal income tax, which are regressive rather than progressive, the total burden of taxes turns out to be effectively proportional to income.[22]

Furthermore, the complexity of tax laws ensures that, within any income class, there is enormous variation in the actual rate of taxes paid. To cite just one example: among the households with incomes between $100,000 and $499,000 in 1971, the average tax rate was 25%; but 1000 households in this group paid less than 6% of their income in taxes, while 22,000 more paid less than 20%.[23]

In short, our tax system is not effectively progressive; it is not even consistently proportional. The actual tax rate a person pays depends on his success in reducing his tax through exclusions and deductions of many kinds, and no matter how large one's income it is possible to pay a very low rate of tax.

These facts are familiar to anyone who has studied the tax system, and perhaps they are not surprising to anyone. I believe they should surprise and even shock us. However, what is most shocking is not the lack of graduation or the variation in individuals' rates but rather the pervasive deceptiveness of the system.

Every taxpayer has eased the pain of paying taxes by looking farther down the tax tables to see how much higher a rate of taxes she would have to pay if her income were higher. These tables deceive us: the complexity of tax law makes actual rates much less progressive than the nominal rates, and the steeply graduated nominal rates provide an incentive to the rich to exploit the available loopholes. But the complexity of the tax laws compels those with modest incomes to pay something near their nominal tax rate, since only a skilled and expensive tax accountant can find all the available loopholes in the maze of laws which apply to the income tax.

The present tax system, then, seems designed to deceive: it supplements nominally progressive rates with a sufficient range of loopholes to ensure that actual rates are scarcely progressive at all. Worst of all, the very deceptiveness of the present system is probably essential to its stability: the rich would not tolerate a tax structure as progressive as the income tax purports to be, while the rest of society would not tolerate a system which openly displayed the favorable treatment it offers the rich.

How could the inequities of the present tax system be remedied? In two ways: we might try to reform the present tax system, and the income tax in particular; or we might substitute a different set of taxes.

Many commissions and individuals have recommended sweeping reforms of the income tax, by broadening the definition of income and by closing many existing loopholes, for example. But even the fairest income tax has important defects. Taxing income is a reasonably effective way of spreading the cost of government, satisfying the first standard of fairness offered above; but it is an indirect and flawed tool for controlling wealth.

High personal income and great wealth are not perfectly correlated; and where they diverge, there are more urgent reasons of justice for limiting wealth than for equalizing income. Wealth, not income, determines one's capacity to spend, and it is the wealthy—even if their current income is modest—who have the greatest ability to exercise political power and undermine political equality. Furthermore, wealth is much more unequally distributed in the United States than is income; much of the wealth of the present generation is inherited; and wealth typically results not from patient effort and prudent saving but from unpredictable economic events.[24]

Therefore, the second assumption mentioned earlier is false: the income tax is not the fairest tax available to us. A personal tax on wealth would better satisfy the standards of fairness in taxation.

Let me conclude by offering an outline of a system of taxes which could satisfy the standards of fairness in taxation. Taxation of wealth would take two forms: a tax on the transfer of wealth, paid by the recipient, and a tax on personal wealth, paid annually (or possibly every two or three years) by the holder. The personal wealth tax would allow an initial exclusion, and only those with substantial holdings would be subject to tax. Its rates would begin very low and would be gently graduated. The net effect of the tax would be to slow the growth of personal fortunes and, assuming that the highest rates are greater than the expected return on investments, virtually to prevent their growth beyond a certain level.

The tax on wealth transfers would also allow an initial exclusion, but rates thereafter would be higher and more steeply graduated. The tax would be a cumulative lifetime accessions tax: the rate of tax would be determined by the total quantity of gifts and bequests received by an individual in his lifetime. (Existing federal gift and inheritance taxes, in contrast, are graduated according to the size of the gift or estate, without regard to the amount given to each recipient.) There are two reasons why these rates should be higher than those of the personal wealth tax: first, gifts and bequests are taxed only once; and second, any reservations we may have about the legitimacy of heavy taxes on personal wealth seem less relevant to inherited or transferred wealth. Transfers or bequests between husband and wife would be exempt from taxation, however, if married couples are to be considered, as now, as a single taxable unit.

Would these taxes force the children of a farm owner, for example, to break up the family farm and sell it to developers in order to pay the taxes on their parents' death? In some cases this might result; and if this is an unacceptable consequence, we ought simply to acknowledge that fact and adjust the tax system accordingly. Perhaps family-owned and family-run farms up to a certain size should be exempted from the wealth transfer tax.

This does not imply that the tax structure I have proposed is unsound; rather, it simply indicates that in some cases other social interests, such as our common interest in preserving farmland, may override the need to limit inequality.

Wealth taxes by themselves probably could not provide sufficient revenue, on a sufficiently predictable schedule, to support government. But if wealth taxes and income taxes are combined, the result is a strong disincentive to save, since savings are taxed as income and may be taxed again as wealth. In place of an income tax, therefore, wealth taxes should be supplemented by a personal consumption tax, based on total personal expenditures. A tax on consumption, complicated as it sounds to administer, amounts to a tax on income minus net savings (plus spending out of previous savings). Here too there would be an initial exclusion: no consumption tax would be due on expenditures which are necessary to provide for basic needs. Past that point the tax might be graduated; or, if the two wealth taxes suffice to limit inequalities, the consumption tax might be a strictly proportional tax. This would offer the advantage of simplicity of assessment and collection and would remove from this tax, at least, the "graduated incentive" for dishonesty.

My proposal, then, is for a set of three taxes which would replace the present federal tax system: a net wealth tax, a wealth transfer tax, and a personal consumption tax. There would be practical difficulties in determining individuals' wealth and consumption, but these do not seem very much greater than the difficulty of determining income.

I have intentionally left the precise working of the system unspecified, since it cannot be determined in the abstract. Actual tax rates to be imposed would depend on many empirical factors: on projected revenue, on the pattern of distribution of wealth, and, more indirectly, on information about the effects of various tax rates on economic activity.

The tax system I have proposed would not be easy to establish or simple to administer. It would, however, be consistent and fair in its operation, and it would satisfy far better than the present system the two standards of equitable distribution of the cost of government and limitation of economic inequality. It is a radical alternative to present structures; though it does not seem to me impractical, it may be unrealistic to consider its actual implementation. But others have also dreamed of a society in which philosophers were rulers and justice was the source of law.[25]

St. Olaf College

NOTES

1. A discussion of this complex issue can be found, for example in Edmund Phelps, "Justice in the Theory of Public Finance," *Journal of Philosophy*, 76: 677-92 (November 1979).

2. I have argued for this definition of coercion in my *Rights and Wrongs: The Justification of Coercion and Punishment* (Selinsgrove, PA: Susquehanna University Press, forthcoming), ch. 2. Cf. Robert Nozick, "Coercion," in Sidney Morgenbesser, Patrick Suppes, and Morton White, eds., *Philosophy, Science, and Method: Essays in Honor of Ernest Nagel* (New York: St. Martin's Press, 1969).

3. Robert Nozick, *Anarchy, State, and Utopia* (New York: Basic Books, 1974), pp. 169-74.

4. Lester Thurow, *The Impact of Taxes on the American Economy* (New York: Praeger Publishers, 1971), p. 140.

5. A brief survey of several senses of horizontal equity, and an account of how these various senses might function in normative tax theory, can be found in A. R. Atkinson, "Horizontal Equity and the Distribution of the Tax Burden," in Henry J. Aaron and Michael J. Boskin, ed., *The Economics of Taxation* (Washington: The Brookings Institution, 1980), pp. 3-18.

6. "Taxation according to ability to pay for the last hundred years or more has been a universally accepted postulate, not only amongst political and economic writers, but amongst the public at large." Nicholas Kalder, *An Expenditure Tax* (London, George Allen and Unwin, 1955), p. 26.

7. William Lucas Sargent, "An Undiscriminating Income Tax Revisited," *Journal of the Statistical Society of London*, vol. 25 (1862), p. 352; quoted in Harold M. Groves, *Financing Government*, 6th edition (New York: Holt, Reinhart and Wilson, 1964), p. 4.

8. John Stuart Mill, remarks before the Select Committee on Income and Property Tax, 1961; quoted in Kaldor, p. 26. Mill believed that progressive taxation of earned income would be "unjust and impolitic," but he did not oppose progressive taxation of unearned income, including progressive taxes on inheritance. See Harold Groves, *The Tax Philosophers* (Madison, WI: University of Wisconsin Press, 1974), pp. 33-34.

9. See, for example, Richard A. Musgrave, *The Theory of Public Finance* (New York: McGraw-Hill Book Co., 1959), p. 96.

10. Thurow, *Impact of Taxes*, p. 140.

11. John Rawls, *A Theory of Justice* (Cambridge: Harvard University Press, 1971), pp. 302 *et passim*.

12. See Thurow, *Impact of Taxes*, p. 147.

13. A fourth alternative, which I do not consider here, is a capitation tax, a tax of so much per person. The defects of such a tax as a source of general revenue are obvious.

14. See C. Harry Kahn, "The Place of Consumption and Net-Worth Taxes in the Federal Tax Structure," in Richard Musgrave, ed., *Broad-Based Taxes: New Options and Sources* (Baltimore: John Hopkins Press, 1973), pp. 133-37, for a brief survey of the alternative bases and kinds of taxation.

15. An international survey of wealth taxes can be found in a study by the Organization for Economic Cooperation and Development, *The Taxation of Net Wealth, Capital Transfers, and Capital Gains of Individuals: Report of the OECD Committee on Fiscal Affairs*, 1979 (Paris: OECD, 1979).

16. Kalder, *An Expenditure Tax*. It was primarily at Kaldor's urging that both India and Sri Lanka introduced expenditure or consumption taxes, and Kaldor was instrumental in drawing up the legislation.

17. See Richard E. Slitor, "Administrative Aspects of Expenditures Taxation," in Musgrave, ed., *Broad-Based Taxes*, pp. 227-29. Several sources mention that the administrative difficulties of collecting a consumption tax in a largely pre-industrial society proved to be prohibitive.

18. Next largest as a source of revenue were payroll taxes (31%), which do not really belong in the category of general taxes since they are paid into a trust fund which supports only one government program. The next largest general tax was the corporate income tax (13% of total revenues), followed by excise taxes (5%) and estate and gift taxes (1%). These are estimates based on partial year information made by the U.S. Treasury Department and Office of Management and Budget; for previous years where full information is available the figures are very similar. See *The World Almanac and Book of Facts 1981* (New York: Newspaper Enterprise Institute, 1981), p. 164.

19. See the official Internal Revenue Service figures in *World Almanac*, p. 103.

20. Joseph Pechman and Benjamin Okner, *Who Bears the Tax Burden?* (Washington: The Brookings Institution, 1974), p. 59. Pechman and Okner's is the most comprehensive study I have found of the actual distribution of taxes. One complication which needs to be mentioned here but has been disregarded in the text: Pechman and Okner consistently provide two or more sets of figures on tax rates based on different sets of assumptions about the effect of *ad rem* taxes. For example, corporate income taxes are paid by corporations, but if they are assumed to be paid by the owners of capital, by stockholders of a corporation, for example, in the form of reduced dividends, the resulting tax distribution appears more progressive than if they are assumed to be paid by consumers, in the form of increased prices. Similarly, property taxes may be assumed to be paid by property owners (the more progressive assumption) or indirectly by renters in the case of rental housing (the less progressive assumption.) The details of these sets of assumptions, and the difficult question of which is the most realistic, are beyond my scope here; the figures given in the text, therefore, are my own averages of Pechman and Okner's "most progressive" and "least progressive" assumptions.

Pechman and Okner's work is based on exhaustive computer analysis of 1966 federal tax returns; I have found no equally thorough study using more recent data. Okner has compared the 1966 results with data from 1970, however, and has found only slight differences in the aspects of tax incidence which he compared. See Okner, "Total U.S. Taxes and Their Effect on the Distribution of Family Income in 1966 and 1970," in Aaron and Boskin, *Economics of Taxation*, pp. 69-84.

One tax incidence study by conservative economists adopted highly progressive incidence assumptions and found that, with these assumptions, the total burden of federal taxes is progressive across most income classes. But even this study found that the *marginal* rate of taxation is regressive as income rises from low to moderately high; the marginal tax rate becomes progressive only at the highest income levels. See Edgar K. Browning and William R. Johnson, *The Distribution of the Tax Burden* (Washington, D.C.: American Enterprise Institute for Public Policy Research, 1979).

21. According to one study, the highest population decile pays only about 10% more of its total income in federal income tax than the lowest decile, and the difference between the second lowest and the second highest decile is less than 7%. See Pechman and Okner, *Tax Burden*, p. 59. The differences stated hold in both the more progressive and the less progressive incidence assumptions.

22. Pechman and Okner, *op. cit.*, pp. 4-10.

23. *Reforming the Federal Tax Structure*, Tables 17 and 35, pp. 204 and 221. These figures were obtained with "full shifting" assumptions, parallel to the "more progressive" assumptions of the Pechman and Okner study; since these figures were given in numbers of households, it was not possible to average the two sets of assumptions. Both sets of assumptions used here showed similar variation in each income class listed.

24. See Lester Thurow, *Generating Inequality: Mechanisms of Distribution in the U.S. Economy* (New York: Basic Books, 1975), chs. 1 and 6.

25. This paper is an excerpt from a paper I wrote as a participant in a National Endowment for Humanities Summer Seminar for College Teachers, and I wish to acknowledge the support of the Endowment and to thank Gertrude Ezorsky for leading the seminar in the context of which the paper was written. I have benefited greatly from comments given to me by Sidney Gendin, Charles R. Beitz, Ronald Yezzi, David Schodt, and Susan B. Hoekema.

JUSTICE AND THE DISTRIBUTION OF PRIMARY CARE PHYSICIANS*

Brian Schrag

In this paper I shall address the issue of what ought to be the demographical and geographical distribution of the current supply of primary care physicians in the United States. I will not be concerned with economic access to such physicians. These issues, though related, can be separated. Ability to pay for services does not ensure geographical access to services and arguments to ensure geographical access may or may not be arguments to ensure economic access to primary care. The question of the proper geographical distribution of primary care is a limited one, but it provides a good point of engagement of larger questions of social justice, social obligations and liberty in the health care sector.

I shall argue that, given the nature of primary care, the proper principle of distribution is one based on need. Given the nature of that need, I shall argue that the distribution pattern of primary care physicians ought to be, in a sense, egalitarian.

Definition of Primary Health Care

By primary care I shall mean that care which involves the following four functions: (1) provides the patient with his or her first-contact care for a medical problem, the first level of personal care in the health system; (2) provides care for the whole person in an illness rather than care which focuses solely on the illness; (3) coordinates, if necessary, various kinds of care required for a patient at a given time; (4) provides for continuity of health care for a person over time. It should be noted that function (1) distinguishes primary health care from public, environmental and occupation health services.[1]

A central feature of primary care is first-contact care. The characteristics of first-contact care require further elaboration since, although first-contact care is not the whole of primary care it is that aspect which distinguishes it from other specialty care, secondary and tertiary care, and (as we shall see) provides one relevant consideration for determining the proper distribution of primary care physicians.

As Edmund Pellegrino notes, the significance of first-contact care resides in the fact that there is a ubiquitous human need for help in dealing with felt needs for medical assistance.[2] The notion of a need for first-contact care is a complex one and denotes several distinct needs. To begin with, the patient comes to the physician because of a felt need for medical assistance. That concern produces anxiety with the attendant need to deal with that anxiety. Dealing with that anxiety is the first step in the healing process. Hence there is (1) a need to share, transfer or discuss the patient's anxiety about a medical event. The presenting patient also has (2) a need for help in distinguishing those felt needs which have no medical base from those which do and a need for help in distinguishing mild from serious illness. In the event of referral there is (3) a need for guidance in identifying the appropriate point of entry in the medical system and for guidance throughout the referral process.

First-contact care is, or should be, designed to respond to those needs. The primary care physician provides an identifiable person in an identifiable place with whom persons in need can share the anxiety of their medical event. The emphasis, at least at the time of first-contact, is on what the patient, not the physician, perceives as a need.

The primary care physician not only provides for these first-contact needs, he also provides for certain other needs for curing and caring. He meets the (4) need for specific treatment for curable disease or refers the patient to the appropriate level for cure and coordinates that care. Where cure is not appropriate he provides for (5) the need for the caring functions of counseling, symptomatic relief, reassurance or education. Finally, the primary care physician fulfills the (6) need for assuming a longitudinal responsibility for an individual's health care over an extended period of time. Given present training, it is reasonable to assume that primary care physicians can care for all common acute and chronic diseases and provide well-child and adult care.[3]

Although other health practitioners such as nurses and physician assistants may play an important role in providing primary health care services, I assume that the primary care physician is the focal point of such care since he/she would seem best fit by training and perspective to adequately integrate all of the above functions.[4]

Given this description of primary care, I shall assume that general practitioners and family practitioners, and to a lesser extent, general pediatricians and general internists are the specialists that best fit the description of primary care physicians. Obstetricians and gynecologists, on the other hand, do not fulfill the criteria. Accordingly, the statistical data on primary care physicians in this paper will refer to only the four specialties specified.

Current Distribution of Primary Care Physicians

The current ratio of primary care physicians to persons in the U.S. is 1:1333.[5] However, there is considerable variation in the geographical distribution of physicians whether one looks at the distribution by state, counties, Health Service Areas, or even within a single urban area. At the state level, in 1978, the ratio of primary care physicians to persons varied from 1:2857 to 1:645 with a median ratio of 1:1818.[6] In 1975, 145 of the nation's 3200 counties had no physician at all. An analysis of the 204 Health Service Areas of the U.S. shows that 142 HSAs have less than their equivalent share of primary care physicians.[7] Manpower shortage areas are areas that have ratios of 1:3500 or less. The number of such areas per state (1978) varied from 0 to 53. States with relatively high numbers of primary care physicians may still have a large number of MSAs.[8] In 1977 only about one-half of towns in the 10-20 thousand population category had an internist and/or pediatrician.[9] In 1976 in metropolitan low income areas, the ratio of primary care physicians to population was 1:7518.[10]

The Proper Distribution of the Current Supply of Primary Care Physicians

Clearly then, whether one looks at the level of urban populations, county populations, Health Service Areas or of individual states, there is a very uneven distribution of primary care physicians. Whether that constitutes a maldistribution and whether we ought to distribute those physicians differently depends upon what is determined to be the most justified distributive principle in this case and what is the most justified public policy on this issue.

In what follows I shall be concerned with one of two distinguishable issues. I shall attempt to determine that principle of distributive justice which is most justifiably invoked for this distribution issue. I will not have time to show what public policy regarding the distribution of primary care physicians is most justified. The justification of a public policy is not solely a search for a justified principle of distribution. Policy justification appropriately takes into account a range of considerations broader than the justice of a distribution, including other moral and political considerations as well as factual features of the situation and of society in general.

A Principle for Just Distribution

The trained services of primary care physicians are a social good produced by the cooperative efforts of society. (By 1976, 560 million dollars in federal funds alone were spent per year for direct support of medical student education specifically to increase the number of primary care physicians.)[11] Given this social good, produced by cooperative effort, by what principle of distribution should the distribution of those physicians be determine?

It is a principle of reason that instances of the same kind ought to be treated in the same way. Hence it is a formal principle of distributive justice that one ought to treat relevantly similar claims to a distributive share in relevantly similar ways. This, of course, leaves unspecified just what characteristics of the distribution situation are to serve as a criterion of relevance.[12] Different material principles of justice will result from the stipulation of different characteristics such as desert, merit, contribution, effort, ability to pay, and need.

How does one rationally justify the selection of a criterion of relevance and hence a principle of distributive justice? As in any enterprise of rational justification, one wishes to avoid arbitrariness. One way to do so is to show that a claimed criterion of relevance derives from a necessary feature of its subject matter and is not merely based on the user's preference or desires. Relevance is a slippery notion, but I shall maintain that there are at least two senses of relevance that ought to be considered in the context of determining a material principle of distributive justice.

First, a characteristic of the distributive situation might be said to be relevant if there is a conceptual 'fit' or appropriateness between that feature and the *nature* of the good to be distributed. Thus, the bravery of a soldier's actions is a conceptually appropriate feature if the good to be distributed is a medal for valour in battle, whereas a soldier's shoe size or income are conceptually inappropriate features.

Secondly, a feature may be said to be relevant in the sense that it is appropriate to the *point* or *purpose* of producing the good to be distributed. Thus if the purpose of creating fire departments is to provide residents with fire protection, then the presence of a fire in a house would be a relevant feature in distributing that fire protection and on the other hand it would be irrelevant, in the sense of pointless, to appeal to house color in the distribution of that protection.

I shall claim that a feature is relevant in determining the selection of a material principle of justice if it is relevant in the sense of being conceptually appropriate to the *nature* of the good being distributed or relevant in the sense of being positively related to the *point* or purpose in producing the good to be distributed.

In the present case the good to be distributed, the service of primary care physicians, is one designed solely to meet a human need for primary care. If the sole function of that good is to satisfy a need for primary health care, then the presence (or absence) of that need is certainly a feature that is conceptually appropriate to the nature of that good and hence is relevant in determining the selection of a material principle of justice. At the same time it would be conceptually odd to completely disregard need for primary care in selecting a distribution principle for a good whose nature it is to satisfy that need. The feature of need is thus relevant in the sense of being conceptually appropriate to the nature of the good being distributed.

Need is also relevant in the sense of being related to the purpose in producing the good. The major, if not only, purpose of society in producing primary care physicians is to satisfy need for primary care. The presence (or absence) of a need for primary care is surely a relevant feature in determining the selection of a distribution principle since it is directly related to the purpose of the good's production.

Since the need of a recipient for primary care is in both senses relevant to the distribution of primary care physicians, any justified principle for the distribution of this good ought to take need into account.

Now it is surely true that the presence of a need does not entail that we ought to produce goods and services to satisfy that need. That is, the presence of need is not necessarily relevant to the allocation of resources for the *production* of a good. However, given that we have already produced a service solely and specifically to satisfy a particular need, then we have sufficient warrant for the claim that such need is a relevant characteristic for determining *distribution* of the good.

Are there any other characteristics which would be necessarily relevant features for a distribution principle in this situation? It is instructive to consider some of the characteristics which presently do causally determine the distribution of primary care physicians in the United States. Those characteristics include the particular population's aggregate wealth, level of education, racial or ethnic make-up and the cultural opportunities and physical attractiveness of the population area.[13]

There are two reasons for rejecting all these characteristics as criteria in a distribution principle. (1) None of these features have any conceptual connection to the *concept* of medical service to satisfy a need for health care or the *point* of producing medical service. Hence, it would be irrational in the sense of appealing to irrelevant and arbitrary characteristics to discriminate between groups on these bases in determining geographical access to primary physician care. (2) Distribution in accordance with any one of them is incompatible with distribution by need which we have already established as relevant. Use of any of these other features would in effect allow those with little or no need in one area to have a level of access to primary care physicians that would be denied to the actually needy in another area. This would be to treat relevantly different cases in relevantly similar ways and that is inconsistent.[14]

Since there is no positive argument for the relevance of such features to the nature of the good being distributed or to the point of producing the good and since appeal to such features would be incompatible with appeal to a feature shown to be relevant, there are strong grounds for rejecting all such features as criteria in a distribution principle for primary health care.

We have considered the most plausible candidates for a criterion of relevance and argued that only one of them can be justified in this situation, viz., need. Hence, the justified principle of distribution can be stated as follows: Distribute primary care physicians to areas in proportion to that area's need for geographical access to primary care physicians. Notice that the actual *pattern* of distribution will be determined by the principle, in conjunction with the characteristics of the need and the degree of need in that area.

To see how an actual pattern of distribution will be determined by the need for primary care, recall the earlier distinction between needs for first-contact care and needs for other aspects of primary care. The needs for first-contact care include: (1) a need to deal with the anxiety of a medical event; (2) a need for help in determining the significance of felt needs; and (3) a need for guidance in the referral process, should that be necessary. I shall argue that these needs have several features which help determine the pattern of distribution.

One such feature of these needs is their universality. We all experience illness or felt needs for medical assistance. We thus all have, at one time or another, a need for first-contact care. If the need is universal, then given that persons with equal needs have equal claims to primary care, it would be unjust to have areas with no access to primary care. Since the need could be universal without being uniformly distributed, this argument can only establish that populations in every area must have *some* access, a condition presently not met in our society. The argument does not establish that primary care physicians ought to be uniformly distributed geographically.

A second, stronger argument to establish such an even distribution of primary care physicians can be stated as follows. (1) The need for first-contact care is an important human need. Illness or perceived illness and the anxiety associated with it reduces our freedom of movement, decision making powers and independence. Hence freedom from illness and its attendant anxiety is a prior condition for the full exercise of our most basic rights or liberties. Few events are more distressing or threatening to our humanity than such a medical event since illness or injury produce a profound anxiety in us regarding what will happen to us and what we should do next. For this reason, illness causes a radical shift in our priorities; the values of other social goods become subservient to a need to be restored to the autonomy made possible by good health. (2) If a need is very important for individuals, and in principle, is very difficult for the individual to provide for themselves, then society ought to provide for the satisfaction of that need. I have argued that the need for first-contact care is such a need. (3) People have an equal claim to satisfy equal need. This follows from the distribution principle already established. (4) Without access to first-contact care, irrespective of geographical location, these equal claims cannot be treated equally. The need for the personal security of medical advice and assistance in first-contact care cannot be met if patients do not have reasonable geographical access to a physician.[16] Excessive distance to a primary care physician not only provides a physical barrier to care but also a psychological one.[17] Hence we have a need for uniform access to first-contact care irrespective of geographical region. Individuals have no practical way of providing that access on their own; hence society has an obligation to ensure that sort of equal access.

A buttressing argument can be given for the second and fourth premises of the above argument. The need for first-contact care is essentially a need for a form of personal security that is very important but cannot in principle be provided for by the individual. It is, in this respect, exactly parallel to the need for fire and police protection. Our society considers those needs sufficiently important and difficult to supply individually that, not only do we provide them, we locate services for them on a roughly even geographical basis in order to ensure equal access to them. Hence, premises (2) and (4) are claims that we actually already accept in other areas of public policy and practice.

A third major argument can be made by appealing to the fact that the need for first-contact care is uniformly distributed throughout the country. Since the incidence of disease is fairly evenly distributed throughout the country, then so is physiologically-based need for first-contact care.[18] One indication of this is that, for those who can get to a physician, the number of office visits *per capita* is about the same throughout the country. If the need is uniformly distributed throughout the general population, irrespective of geographical location, then access to primary care should not vary by geographical area.

One can also argue for uniform distribution by consideration of the efficiency of the medical system. A medical system ought to be designed to efficiently meet the medical needs of the population. If first-contact service, which serves as the major entry point into the system, is not uniformly distributed throughout the population while need is, then in some areas serious medical problems will needlessly go undetected or treated while in other areas less serious illness will be give disproportionate attention. This is not an efficient use of the medical system.

Finally, need for other aspects of primary care also provide a similar argument for an even distribtuion of primary care physicians. If the incidence of common diseases is distributed in a roughly even manner throughout the country, then the need for the curing and caring functions of primary care will also be fairly evenly distributed. Hence there ought to be a uniform *per capita* distribution of primary care physicians.

I have argued that the use of a need-based principle of distribution will, given certain features of those needs, as a contingent matter of fact yield a roughly egalitarian pattern of distribution. The pattern is not simply an equal distribution of physicians per acre nor simply a uniform distribution by population. It must be a distribution that provides at least roughly uniform geographical access throughout the population. It should be noted that since the distribution principle is need based, if there are identifiable areas in which there is a demonstrable physiologically based need for a greater *per capita* concentration of primary care physicians, then that allocation ought to be made.[19] Since it is the roughly egalitarian *pattern* of distribution that is relevant to the following discussion, I shall for convenience, refer to the principle as an egalitarian principle.

Even if an egalitarian pattern is *prima facie* justified, there are side constraints on a justifiable principle of distribution. Whether a distribution principle is justified will depend, in part, upon the degree of scarcity of the good being distributed. Suppose a quantity of food is divided among a population according to an apparently just principle of distribution but the resultant portions are less than required to sustain life. Here everyone receives a fair share but everyone's share is below some minimally acceptable level. Such a distribution may be just but it is not wise. Everyone will starve. If the good to be distributed is that scarce, what Rescher calls an economy of dire insufficiency,[20] then a more appropriate distribution principle would be one that presses only the minimum number of people below a minimally acceptable level.[21] In an economy of mere insufficiency, on the other hand, there may not be enough of the good to satisfy everyone's legitimate claims but the distribution principle does not push anyone below the floor of an acceptable minimum. In such an economy, the otherwise justified principle of distribution should hold. In industrialized countries such as England and the United States, a primary care physician-to-population ratio of 1:3000 is considered barely minimal by physicians and policy makers. The United States, with its current primary care physician-to-population ratio of 1:1333 is surely at least in the latter category and hence the egalitarian distribution principle should be retained.

Another constraint on a principle of distribution has to do with the principle's impact on the production of the good to be distributed. Thus if an otherwise justified principle of distribution adversely affects the production of the good so that shares of individual recipients are less than they would be under an alternative scheme, the principle ought not to be adopted.

One might argue that an egalitarian distribution scheme for primary care physicians in the United States would make the practice of medicine so unattractive to students and the total supply would be so diminished that the physician-population ratio would be lower than it is for the worst-off population under the current free market system. Since the ratio of the primary care physicians for that worst-off population is presently in the neighborhood of 1:7500, that is not a realistic expectation. One might also note that in England much more stringent restrictions on physician liberty than are contemplated here accompanied the introduction of the National Health Service. There the number of applicants to medical school did not decline but in fact increased until it was determined in the mid 1960's to cut back the enrollments in medical schools.[22] Furthermore, given the relatively high income of physicians, some limitation on practice location is not likely to have much effect on production.

Any negative effect might well be further reduced by the methods used to achieve an egalitarian distribution. It is true that those methods will have to go somewhat farther in restricting the liberty of physicians than the methods tried so far in the United States, of trying to attract doctors to underserved areas by building and modernizing hospitals there, and of paying educational costs for medical students in exchange for 1-5 years service in those areas after they qualify.[23] These methods have been quite ineffective.[24] Yet methods that interfere with liberty very little are available; among them are making new licenses to practice available for a time only in underserved areas and making service in such areas for a period of 4 years or more a condition of admission to medical schools. These measures require no more than a fair return for the massive public subsidies given medical education. To those who would still object on grounds of liberty one might reply by asking if it is so intuitively obvious that waiving any demand for a fair return, in deference to the preferences of 167,000 primary care physicians (actually of a much smaller number of recruits to this body), can outweigh the health and perhaps lives of the 40 to 50 million people in this country who are medically underserved? One might also note that good health is a causally prior condition for much exercise of liberty. Hence liberty has to be considered on the side of the patients, too.

I should like to comment on the method of justification that has been employed in this paper. The process of rational justification as I understand it is an attempt to avoid arbitrariness in one's beliefs. Consequently, in determining the appropriate distribution principle one ought to avoid the evil of a purely subjective approach or the random, *ad hoc* method of analysis of situation ethics.

The standard approach is to justify a particular distribution principle by showing that it can be deduced from what Ruth Macklin calls the "global" theories of social justice, viz. utilitarianism, egalitarianism, libertarianism, and a Rawlsian theory.[25] There are several difficulties with this approach. To begin with, there is difficulty in determining the correct way to interpret global theory for application to a particular area such as health care.[26] Partly for this reason, global theories do not seem to yield a determinate solution for particular distribution problems of social policy. Furthermore, as Macklin has noted, no one has yet given a knock-down argument in favor of one of the global theories. Hence it is not likely that widespread agreement and support for a policy will be obtained simply by showing that the policy can be deduced from one of the theories. It will be very difficult to persuade opponents that the policy does not rest ultimately on a personal preference for one of the theories. Finally, it is not clear that, in the resolution of practical problems, consistency requires that one specify, in advance, all the relevant values to be considered in all issues of distribution. This is essentially what one does in choosing a global theory and applying it to all cases of social justice.[27]

Given my dissatisfaction with the standard approach and in order to avoid the subjectivist approach, I have tried to justify a principle of distribution that is appropriate to the nature of the good to be distributed, yet consistent with the factual situation. Since the scope of the application of the principle is restricted to a fairly narrow range of goods, i.e., goods clearly designed to meet needs, this increases the likelihood of gaining public acceptance for the principle. It leaves people free to disagree on other distribution issues while accepting this principle. Hence the likelihood is increased of getting agreement on a policy deduced from this principle compared to the standard approach.

Justifying a Distribution Policy

The question of how primary care physicians should be distributed in our society is not solely a search for a justified principle of distribution. Even if we have established what would be a just distribution pattern, that does not settle the issue of whether it ought to be adopted as a public policy. Here one may have to weigh the value of a just distribution against conflicting values and consider other values and facts about the nature of health care and society. Neither does it settle the issue of specifically how such a policy is to be implemented. Such considerations are, unfortunately, beyond the scope of this paper.

Hampden-Sydney College

NOTES

*I gratefully acknowledge helpful discussion of some of the ideas in this paper by all my colleagues in an NEH year-long seminar for 1981-82 and especially to Steven Lammers, David Newell, Robert Rhodes and David Smith.

1. For a discussion of definitions of primary care see E. Pellegrino and D. Thomasma, *A Philosophical Basis of Medical Practice*. (Oxford: Oxford University Press, 1981), pp. 234-35. Also C. Roddy "Need Based Requirements of Primary Care Physicians," *JAMA* January 24, 1980, vol. 243, no. 4, p. 355.

2. This characterization of first-contact care and its moral significance that is developed in the following paragraphs is drawn from Pellegrino, *op. cit.*, p. 235-36.

3. Roddy, *op. cit.*, p. 355.

4. Since the issue here is the distribution of the current supply of primary care physicians, the issue of substitutability of other health practitioners for physicians is not crucial. In a discussion of the most justified total supply of primary care physicians in the U.S., such an issue is appropriate.

5. *Forecasts of Physician Supply and Requirements*. Office of Technology Assessment, (Washington, D.C., April 1980), p. 32.

6. See the Institute of Medicine, *A Manpower Policy for Primary Care*, National Academy of Sciences, (Washington, D.C., May 1978), p. 52.

7. Graduate Medical Education National Advisory Committee (GMENAC) Staff Paper, "Supply and Distribution of Physicians and Physician Extenders," U.S. Department of Health, Education and Welfare. Bureau of Health Manpower 1978, DHEW Publications No (HRA) 78-11, pp. 45-46.

8. See The Institute of Medicine, *A Manpower Policy for Primary Care*, p. 11.

9. W. B. Schwartz, *et al.*, "The Changing Geographical Distribution of Board-Certified Physicians," *New England Journal of Medicine*, (October 30, 1980), vol. 303, no. 18, p. 1032.

10. *Forecasts, op. cit.*, p. 37.

11. This does not include support for capital outlays, medical research or patient treatment. Nor does it include individual state support. For a summary of the federal role in the financing of training of physicians see, R. Scheffler, *et al.*, "Physicians and New Health Practitioners: Issues for the 1980's." *Institute of Medicine*, National Academy of Sciences, (Washington, D.C., May 1979), p. 1.

12. As J. L. Lucas observes, "We do well to replace controversies about equality by arguments about criteria of relevance or irrelevance." J. L. Lucas, *The Principles of Politics*, (Oxford, 1966).

13. P. Knox. "Medical Deprivation, Area Deprivation and Public Policy," *Social Science and Medicine*, vol. 13D, p. 111. See also M. Woolf, *et al.*, "Demographic Factors Associated with Physician Staffing in Rural Areas: The Experience of the National Health Service Corps," p. 449.

14. Other standard criteria of justice, such as ability, merit, effort, socially useful service, and contribution do not seem to work in this connection. Contribution, for example, cannot be limited to current financial contributions to medical education. If, however, past contributions and contributions other than financial ones are included, the criterion becomes unmanageably complicated.

15. In what follows, the first two major arguments are either reconstructions of arguments made by Pellegrino or suggested by his arguments, *op. cit.*, pp. 234-41.

16. For a definition of reasonable access, see *Forecasts, op. cit.*, pp. 82-83.

17. Knox, *op. cit.*, p. 115. See also P. Gober and R. Gordon, "Intraurban Physician Location: A Case Study of Phoenix," *Social Science and Medicine*, vol. 14D, pp. 415-16.

18. "Acute Conditions: Incidence and Associated Disabilities U.S. July 1977-June 1978," *Vital and Health Statistics*, Series 10, no. 132. U.S. DHEW, pub. no. HRA 79-1560. (HRA Rockville, Md., September 1979), p. 6.

19. G. Silver, "Reply to Professor Bryant," *International Journal of Health Services*, vol. 7, no. 4, (1977), p. 724.

20. N. Rescher, *Distributive Justice*, (Bobbs-Merrill Company, Inc., 1966), p. 96.

21. Rural areas of developing countries would be examples of an economy of dire insufficiency. There the ratio of physicians to population typically range from 1:25,000 to 1:500,000. See J. Bryant, *Health and the Developing World*, (Cornell University Press, Ithaca, 1972).

22. Knox, *op. cit.*, p. 114.

23. The first of the two approaches mentioned was taken in the Hill-Burton Act of 1946. The second approach was taken in a variety of subsequent federal programs, including the National Health Service Corporation.

24. See L. J. Clarke *et al.*, "The Impact of Hill-Burton: An Analysis of Hospital Bed and Physician Distribution in the United States, 1950-1970," *Medical Care*, May 1980, vol. XVIII, no. 5. On the other approach, see M. Woolf, "Demographic Factors Associated with Physician Staffing in Rural Areas: The Experience of the National Health Service Corps," *Medical Care*, April 1981, vol. XIX, no. 4., as well as Clarke, *op. cit.*, p. 546.

25. Ruth Macklin, "Public Policy and Health Care: An Egalitarian Approach to Dilemmas of Distributive Justice." Read at Hampden-Sydney College, March 1979.

26. For a careful analysis of four attempts to apply Rawls' theory to health care, see Norman Daniels, "Rights to Health Care and Distributive Justice: Programmatic Worries." *The Journal of Medicine and Philosophy*, (1979), vol. 4, no. 2.

27. For an interesting discussion of the relation of the specification of values to the justification of practical policy, see R. M. Hare, "Contrasting Methods of Environmental Planning," in *Nature and Conduct*, (St. Martin's Press, 1975).

MUST ONE HAVE THE CONSENT OF AN ORGAN DONOR?

Hardy Jones

Organ transplantation is an increasingly useful means of prolonging life and alleviating suffering. Under what conditions is the practice justified? One familiar, widely-accepted, view is that its acceptability is dependent upon the consent of the person from whose body the organ is extracted. The strongest version of this "consent view" is that transplantation is justifiable if and only if the donor gives his or her consent. Perhaps few would accept the presumably less defensible half of this biconditional — that the consent of the donor is a sufficient moral condition for donation, extraction, and transplantation. Though there are good reasons for rejecting the claim, I do not delineate them here. Instead I consider the more plausible contention that consent of the "loser" of a bodily part is a necessary condition for the moral permissibility of taking it in order to help someone else. I argue that this claim is false.

I

It is useful to consider a few hypothetical cases — ones unlikely to arise in actual medical practice. First, suppose that approximately one-half of the human population were born with three kidneys and the other half were born with one kidney. Suppose that everyone needs two kidneys, and only two kidneys, in order to live and to be healthy. In this bizarre world extraction and re-implantation can be performed with little pain, minimal inconvenience, and no serious risk to life and well-being. One would hope and expect, of course, that enough three-kidneyed persons would voluntarily come forward to donate. But what if coerced takings were necessary in order to prevent otherwise certain, early death to many people? This could be plausibly regarded as a way of forcing persons to fulfill an obligation of minimal beneficence to their fellow human beings.

Suppose there were a human organ that only women need — without it they are doomed to a short life of intense pain. Their need arises when they reach the age of twenty-one. For men, however, this organ is superfluous — it is no more important than the useless appendices in the present world. In the imaginary world approximately half of all females are born without it, but all males are born with it. Suppose further that, as in the previous case, removal and transplantation can be accomplished with a minimum of personal and financial costs. These circumstances seem to warrant compulsory donation just in case there are too few men who are willing to donate. Suppose that many men refuse for reasons that are merely selfish or petty. Aren't the overwhelmingly serious needs of the women of such importance that any obligation not to compel donation is defeated or overridden?

Consider a third example. Suppose that bodily parts such as nails and hair were discovered to be useful for making a drug vitally important in the treatment of cancer. People probably would donate in large numbers. But what if there were not enough? Suppose that too many persons choose to keep or throw away their nails and hairs after cutting. They zealously collect the detritus as it falls from the shears of the barber and the clippers of the manicurist. Surely the relief of suffering and the delay of death from a disease such as cancer would be sufficiently important to warrant forced removal of quarter-inch slivers of those useless parts of the body.

These cases are obviously far-fetched and unrealistic. But they are suggestive of certain important limits on any supposed right to control one's body and to retain one's bodily parts. In all three sets of circumstances it is arguable that one does not have a right to keep what one does not need. If this is correct, then at least one otherwise strong basis for regarding consent as necessary is removed. In none of the examples is there a threat of injury, suffering, or death to the donors. It would seem that consent is most important when there is some such threat or a probability of some other serious loss.

These points are relevant to any judicious consideration of a right that has received much attention in recent discussions of abortion — the right to the use of one's body. Judith Thomson and others have suggested that such a right may be invoked in order to justify abortion of a fetus who has not been given the right to use the pregnant woman's body.[1] Whether or not it is correct, this claim derives much of its plausibility from attention to certain familiar facts about the phenomena of pregnancy and birth in human beings. But what if pregnancy were very different? Suppose there were no pain, no inconvenience, no threat to health, no change in the size of one's body. Suppose that fetuses were borne and born with no attendant difficulties in the lives of adults. Under these conditions, would a pregnant woman — or anyone else — have a right to destroy the fetus on the grounds of a right to the use of one's body? It would seem not. If this is right, surely the best explanaion is that the fetus's use of one's body poses no loss or threat of loss.

Consider a different example. Suppose that A, an attacker, wants to kill V, a victim. A has a gun, and A searches for V. When the attacker finds the victim, he discovers that V is standing behind S and using S's body as a kind of shield. A does not want to risk injury or death to S and will not shoot as long as there is any such danger. In this situation V, who is wholly innocent of any wrongdoing that would justify his being shot, is fully protected as long as S stays where he is. Also, S suffers no serious losses from remaining where he is until the police arrive to arrest A. Suppose that A, V, and S know all of these facts. Would it be permissible for S to move aside and thus expose V's body to A's murderous efforts? It would seem not. S would be wrong to invoke some alleged right to the use of his own body, when this right is construed as a right to prevent V from making use of his (S's) body. The lack of risk to S and the enormous need of V combine, under these circumstances, to make it wrong for S to move aside. The fact that S has not consented to V's use of his body does not make it right for him to allow V to be murdered.

The proper function of consent is to enable persons to protect themselves from infringements of such rights as the rights not to be made to suffer, not to be killed, not to be injured, not to be disabled. The right to retain one's bodily parts is neither absolute nor fundamental. It is derivative from these other more important rights. Indeed, there may not even be a right to the use of one's body or to the retention of one's bodily parts. There may only be rights to certain valuable things sometimes threatened by one's use of one's body or bodily parts—health, security, and life, for instances. When others are in need and the prospective donor is not in need—and where no more basic right is threatened—the "right to retain one's bodily parts" does not stand alone as a bar to compulsory extraction. This alleged right is conditional on there being some significant cost to the donor in losing whatever is taken. It is difficult to judge just how great this cost would have to be. Fortunately, no such estimate is required for the theoretical purposes to which we are now restricted. (It is perhaps worth noting that acceptance of the points illustrated by the examples does not require commitment to any utilitarian view. One need not hold, for instance, that the compulsory donation is justified so long as the total benefits are greater than the total losses, however great these are in the life of the donor.)

II

Dead bodies are extremely valuable for extending life and improving health. Cadavers are needed for experimental and educational purposes.

Also, surgeons can transplant organs and thereby restore sight, diminish pain, and save lives. (In some cases there is a rather ghoulish dimension to this phenomenon. One of my students recently said, "I have a friend who very badly needs a kidney transplant. She's waiting for the motorcycle season to start." A big guy in a black leather jacket stomped out of the room. Toward motorcycle driving and other suicidal acts, they have a tolerant attitude, a sort of "live and let live" attitude.) Does the use of a dead body require the consent of the person who once occupied it? Does a person have a right to absolute control of the use and/or disposal of his or her body after death?

Under the provisions of the Uniform Anatomical Gift Act, a person may, while still alive of course, make a commitment and express a desire that his or her body be used for medical purposes. The family's consent is not needed, and the objections of loved ones are not to be allowed to interfere. Now it seems clear that persons should be informed of this opportunity and be encouraged to give their pre-mortem consent. Presumably there is a right, perhaps even an obligation, to help others in this way. If there is such a right—and especially if it is linked to an obligation, therefore not merely supererogatory—there ought to be assurance that the wish will be respected. There are, however, obvious and serious disadvantages to such a program. It is inadequate, and is likely to continue to be inadequate, to yield enough needed bodily parts. And there is a danger that, as it becomes generally accepted, many people will think of it as the only acceptable way of obtaining needed organs from cadavers.

Should doctors be required to have the prior permission of the deceased in order to proceed with organ extraction to help others? I believe the right answer is "No." If the deceased had expressed no wish one way or another, why should there be a presumption that he or she was opposed or would have been opposed had the issue been confronted? One of course takes a chance that one acts contrary to his or her wishes, but one also takes such a chance by declining to use the body for medical purposes. In a way it is more "respectful" to practice what some have, perhaps derisively, called "routine salvaging." One can do so in the hope that the deceased wanted, or would have wanted, or was not opposed to a humane and beneficial use of the body that he or she no longer needs. (I assume that any loving god would supply to heavenly residents whatever bodily parts they need for whatever joys they can experience. He would give them wings, for example.)

But what if one knows that the person had expressly refused to give permission? Is it permissible to take the organs? The answer would presumably be a clear "No" if the need were not considerable—if, for instance, an organ from another source could be obtained with slightly more inconvenience or somewhat greater cost. But, as we know, the need is often enormous. If a kidney or a heart from a cadaver can prolong life or restore health, must one refrain from using it because of opposition from the person, now dead, who once "owned" the body? Fulfillment of an obligation of beneficence would involve helping others in terrible need when one can do so at little cost to oneself. Surely persons do not need their organs after death. It is difficult to see what one "loses" by having an organ extracted from his or her corpse. The person is no longer alive to lose anything at all—certainly not to experience adverse effects of a loss.[2] So it is at least reasonable to believe donation of one's dead body to be an important way to fulfill an obligation of beneficence. Routine salvaging schemes would simply require persons to do so.

I do not wish to suggest that all who refuse to donate are callous or selfish. But consider the following sentiments: "I know that my body contains organs that prolong life, restore health, and relieve suffering. I know that human beings could benefit enormously from this body. I know also that, being dead, I will have no uses for any of these bodily parts. I know that if the body is buried in the ground, all the organs will rot away. But I refuse to donate; I want my body left untouched by doctors. It is not that I need it or want it for myself after death. Of course, there will be no person there to have needs or wants. Still, I do not want the organs to be transplanted so as to improve anyone's life. I do not want anyone to be helped." Now it seems to me that *this* position is in need of justification. Indeed, the burden of justification seems to be on the one who refuses to donate—not on recipients and doctors who wish to make use of cadavers. Must we respect the view of the refuser? Is there not a moral requirement not to be that sort of person? Must we respectfully submit to wishes that are at variance with that requirement?

III

The position that I have advanced is susceptible to several objections. I shall respond to three. The first involves property rights. The right to refuse to donate is thought to be based on the right to control one's property, as in a will. Respecting a wish not to be a cadaver donor is regarded as akin to respecting a will's provisions for the disposition of a decedent's money or land. As suggested before, however, there appear to be limits to the respect to which such wishes are entitled. Suppose a person has willed that her house be allowed to decay and that no measures are to be taken for its preservation. Or suppose that someone has willed that a million dollars of his cash be placed in a trunk and thrown into the Atlantic Ocean. Surely we have no overriding obligation to carry out such wishes. I suggest that the wish to have one's body placed in a cemetery (or a crematorium, or a mausoleum) is closely analogous. There are limits as to what one may have done with one's property or one's body when no longer able to use and enjoy them.

Compulsory donations of bodily parts may be regarded as a form of redistribution of health. A person's good health or poor health is to a large extent due to factors over which he or she has no control. It is a matter of good luck or bad luck. With respect to wealth, similar factors are plausibly regarded as providing a basis for restrictions on inheritance. Analogously, it seems reasonable to restrict one's disposal of one's body and its parts. (And, as we know, there are those who feel greater intimacy with their oil wells than with their bodily parts.)

The next objection is from Paul Ramsey. In his book, *The Patient as Person*, he says that routine salvaging would be bad because it would deprive people of the opportunity to be generous.[3] He thinks it better—for the development of virtues of kindness and compassion—to have a system of *giving* and *receiving*, rather than one of *taking*. I have three replies. First, one may have a motive of generosity even when the action expressive of generous feeling is morally and legally obligatory. And a recognition of the obligation need not stifle or suppress caring impulses. A law requiring persons to drive safely need not—and most likely does not—stop people from wanting, because of care and concern, not to endanger others while driving. Second, in a world as miserable as ours, there are inexhaustible opportunities to be generous, caring, giving, and loving. There are many other ways besides donation of one's body to care for human beings. Third, even if there would be less generosity with a system of routine salvaging, surely the gains in human betterment easily outweigh the loss. With the lower level of suffering there would be less need for generosity. (The objection is reminiscent of the view that a certain segment of society should be left wretched so that the rich and the healthy can develop their virtues of benevolence.) Compare two worlds, equal in value and disvalue in every way except for disparities as regards suffering and generosity. In W_1, there is extensive suffering in wide variety; but here is also much generosity directed at the sufferers. In W_2, there is no suffering whatsoever; but there is no generosity either. Clearly, W_2 is rationally and morally preferable to W_1.

The last objection is more difficult. What of those who would suffer now and until they die from an awareness that their wishes (to be buried and not to be cadaver donors) will not be respected? How is this suffering to be avoided? It could of course be avoided by restricting outselves to UAGA-type schemes. But this renunciation of routine salvaging would involve tremendous waste of beneficial health resources. Far too few persons sign the donor card or otherwise give consent. There would be earlier deaths, longer suffering, more intense pain, unhappier lives. An alternative plan would be to lie to those who object, assure them that their bodies will not be used, but then harvest the cadavers anyway. An obvious defect here is that, even were this morally acceptable on other grounds, it would be virtually impossible to keep the deception secret. The plan would be self-defeating, and the suffering would be accentuated.[4]

Another device would be to institute a class of exceptions to routine salvaging. Perhaps a person would have to present his or her objections before a panel. He or she would have to show how and why he or she would suffer unless given assurance that the body would not be harvested. Presumably there would have to be *real suffering* — a mild feeling of disgust or repulsion would not be enough. This proposal could be combined with a counseling/educational program through which persons could be assisted in ridding themselves of false or unreasonable beliefs that contribute to their suffering. Appearances before the board of inquiry might be embarrassing, but this would perhaps increase the probability that only sincere sufferers would be unwilling to donate under routine salvaging.[5]

University of Nebraska-Lincoln

NOTES

1. See Judith Thomson, "A Defense of Abortion," *Philosophy and Public Affairs*, Vol. 1, No. 1, Fall, 1971, pp. 47-66.

2. In his article, "Death," Thomas Nagel has forcibly argued that one can endure serious losses and harms that one does not experience. For instance, loss of reputation or esteem. If one does not accept this, it is difficult to maintain that death itself is bad for the person who dies. It remains to be shown, of course, how the extraction of organs from one's cadaver contrary to one's wishes constitutes any harm that outweighs the desperate needs of living persons. See Thomas Nagel, "Death" in *Mortal Questions*, Cambridge University Press, 1979, pp. 1-10. (Originally published in *Noûs*, IV, No. 1, February, 1970.)

3. Paul Ramsey, *The Patient as Person*, Yale University Press, 1971, pp. 198-215, especially pp.210-11.

4. It might, of course, be possible to preserve secrecy in an isolated or unusual case— perhaps one in which there had been a sincere intention not to harvest the body. If at death, the need for an organ were especially acute, it might be furtively excised before burial.

5. Cf. James L. Muyskens, "An Alternative Policy for Obtaining Cadaver Organs for Transplantation," *Philosophy and Public Affairs*, Vol. 8, No. 1, Fall, 1978, pp. 88-89.

LIBRARY OF DAVIDSON COLLEGE

Books on regular loan may be checked out for **two weeks**. Books must be presented at the Circulation Desk in order to be renewed.

A fine is charged after date due.

Special books are subject to special regulations at the discretion of the library staff.